D0129314

Splish, Splash

Water Fun for Kids

Penny Warner

Illustrated by Sean O'Neill

CHICAGO REVIEW PRESS

Library of Congress Cataloging-in-Publication Data

Warner, Penny
    Splish, splash : water fun for kids / Penny Warner. — 1st ed.
      p.   cm.
    ISBN 1-55652-262-2
    1. Water—Recreational use. 2. Games. 3. Amusements. I. Title.
GV191.67.W3W35 1996
797.2'5—dc20   95-40973
                                                CIP

The author and the publisher of this book disclaim all liability in connection with the use of the information contained in this book.

First edition
Published by Chicago Review Press, Incorporated
814 North Franklin Street
Chicago, Illinois 60610
ISBN 1-55652-262-2
Printed in the United States of America

5 4 3 2 1

To my husband, Tom, and my children, Matthew and Rebecca

Contents

Introduction xi

1 Pool and Lake 1

Marco Polo 2
Water Basketball 3
Gold Diggers 4
Butterfingers Ball 6
Frogman—Jump or Dive! 8
Water Volleyball 9
Shipwreck 11
Water Relays 13
Keep It Dry 15
Duck, Duck, Shark! 16
Save Our Ship 17
Jaws 18

2 Ocean and Beach 21

Jai Alai 22
Sea Scope 24
Ice-Water Relay 25
A Beach Party 26
Sand Castles and Sea Shapes 27
Dino Dig 29
Sand-Casting 31
Sandpainting 33
Sand Candles 34
Follow the Pirate 36

3 Kiddie Pool 37

Splash Machine 38
Shark Bait 39
Buried Treasure 40
Frog Invasion 41
Walnut Ships 43
Pop the Piranha 45
Frogs on a Lily Pad 47
Gone Fishing 48
Don't Get Wet! 49
Kiddie Carnival 50

4 Slides, Sprinklers, and Soakers 53

Slippery Slide 54
Erupting Volcano 56
Attack of the Flying Sponges 57
Super Squirter 59
Water Weenie 60
Snake in the Grass 62
Water Olympics 63
Diver Down 65
Game-Show Hose 67
Shooting Gallery 68

5 Bathtub Fun 69

Water Wuppet 70
Spongies 72
Thunderstorm 73
Pirate Ship 74
Sticker Magic 76
Body Paints 78
Icebergs 79
Tub Buddies 81
Soap Shapes 83
Hair Salon 84

6 Water Table 85

Billions of Bubbles 86
Undersea City 89
Water Wax Museum 90
It's Not Water! 91
Sand and Water Wheel 93
Baby Bath 94
Rainy Day Sandbox 95
Watercolors 96
Underwater Bouquet 97

7 Water Activities 99

Birdbath 100
Ice Sculpture 101
Water Music 103
Ice Balloons 104
Ice Caves 106
Frozen Slushies 107
Dancing Water Bugs 109
Water Paints 110
Musical Mud Puddles 111
Creeping Colors 112

8 Water Toys 113

Squirt Bird	114
Ocean Wave Bottle	115
Street Cleaner	117
Water Clock	119
Water Whirlers	120
Snow Globe	121
Rickety Raft	122
Bobbing Boats	124
Magnifying Microscope	126
Water Drum	127

9 Water Games 129

Octopus Tag	130
Swimmy Says	131
Wet T-shirt Race	133
Water Bomb Toss	134
Sinking Ship	136
Splash!	137
Volley Jaws	138
Alligator Escape	140
Sea Hunt	141
Submarine Sonar	142

10 Water Arts and Crafts 145

Soap and Water Crayons	146
Squeeze Paint	147
Sponge Painting	148
Chalk Melt	149
Water Art	150
Rainy Daze	151
Water Sculpture	152
Rainbow Tie-Dye	153
Crystal Art	154
Fire and Ice Candles	155

ACKNOWLEDGMENTS

So many of my child development and special education students at Diablo Valley College, Chabot College, and Ohlone College helped with ideas for this book. I want to thank them all for their contributions: Ryan Brushey, Judy Carbone, Ann Diddy, Teri Dunkin, Adam Galati, Sara Havercroft, Melodi Holden, Laurie Jarocki, Jill Jeffreys, Ruth McAvoy, Kathy Nevins, Jennifer Ostraco, Lya Pires, Shannon Smith, and Allison Stone.

Thanks to the kids who tried out all the water activities and made sure they were fun: Chad Anderson, Craig Clemetson, Jason Cosetti, Jonathan Ellington, Steven Ellington, Brian Hurley, Geoffrey Pike, Jim Russell, Brie Saunders, Brooke Saunders, Kelli Saunders, Kristin Saunders, Sean Saunders, Sue Stadelhofer, Jana Swec, Joseph Swec, Tim Swec, Mia Thiele, Samuel Valdez, Zachary Valdez, Alexander Warner, Nicholas Warner, and Dakota Webster.

Thanks to my writing group: Jonnie Jacobs, Peggy Lucke, Lynn MacDonald, and Sally Richards.

A special thanks to Heather Thornton for coming up with great book ideas.

And a very special thanks to my agent, Lyle Steele, and to my editor, Amy Teschner, for giving me the opportunity to write such a fun and creative book.

INTRODUCTION

Water, water, everywhere—and what fun it is for kids! It's slippery and soggy, wet and wild, and it keeps the kids cool in the summer heat.

All you need to beat the heat and have fun in the sun is some water and a copy of *Splish, Splash*. This ultimate water-play book is chock-full of ideas for games, activities, crafts, and toys for the pool, lake, beach, and backyard. The kids will have a blast!

Splish, Splash offers more than 120 fun-in-the-sun water frolics for kids, from toddlers to teenagers. You'll be surprised how quickly a hose or bucket of water can turn kids of all ages into laughing, fun-loving water worshippers.

Each chapter in *Splish, Splash* describes all kinds of creative ways to have fun with water. There are games to play in the pool, adventures to try in the lake, and suggestions for splashin' in the swimmin' hole. Or you can head for the beach, the shore, or the ocean, and watch the kids kick up the sand while the surf's up. The activities offer tips on suggested ages for play, number of players needed, materials required, object of the water game or activity, and easy-to-follow instructions on how to play or what to do, as well as variations on each offering, for even more water ideas.

No pool? No beach? No problem. For little ones, fill up the plastic kiddie pool—they come in all sizes—and let the tiny tykes wallow in the shallow water. You'll be surprised how much fun even big kids can have in the kiddie pool.

Or turn on the sprinklers, spread out the slides, and shower kids of all ages with soakers, sprayers, and squirters. There's lots of fun to be had outside on the grass. And if it's time to come inside for a bath, even kids who balk at the bathtub will flip and float in their bathtub water world.

And that's not all. You'll find dozens of ideas for water-table fun, plus water activities, toys, games, and even arts and crafts.

Get ready!

Get set!

Get wet!

SAFETY

Safety Tips and Guidelines

Since water play is often slippery, it can be hazardous if it's not properly supervised. The best way you can help prevent the kids from being injured during water play is to watch them closely while they splash and swim. Remember, the more water they play with, the more you'll need to supervise them. To help you know what to watch for, read the safety tips for each activity. Here are some general tips to keep in mind for water-play safety:

• Always supervise the children around water. Do not leave them unattended for a minute, even in the bathtub.

• Remind kids not to run on slippery surfaces, unless it's a soft lawn that won't cause injury if the kids fall down.

- Check with kids to see who can swim and who can't. Don't rely on their word only, however. See for yourself.
- Have kids play games in the shallow end of a lake or pool, so they can always touch the bottom.
- Set rules and guidelines at the beginning of water play so kids know what's safe and what isn't. If they break the rules, have them sit out for a short time, until they're ready to cooperate.
- Remind kids not to splash or squirt each other in the face. They may swallow water or get it in their eyes.
- Tell kids the water they're using for play is not drinking water, unless it comes out of the hose. Provide drinking water separately, or offer the kids other beverages for refreshment.
- Have kids dress appropriately for water play so they won't worry about getting their clothes wet.
- Provide sun protection lotion so kids don't get sunburned. Reapply it often, since most brands wash off. For extra protection, you might even offer them hats and sunglasses, and have them wear their shirts.
- Have extra towels on hand for the kids who forget to bring their own.
- Ask kids to bring waterproof shoes for beach and lake play, in case there are hazards in the water or the sand is hot.
- Inner tubes, air mattresses, inflated toys, and other flotation devices do not offer children safety in the water, so be sure to supervise them.

CHAPTER ONE

The pool, lake, and swimming hole offer lots of ways to have fun in the water. Kids can play on top of the water, under the water, or submerged halfway in between, where they can touch the bottom. In this chapter, you'll find some traditional games to play in the pool, as well as variations on the old favorite, Marco Polo. There are new games to try, too, such as Jaws, Butterfingers Ball, and Shipwreck.

The pool is clean and predictable, but the lake and swimming hole can be uneven and hazardous. Warn kids about the deep areas, and have them wear foot coverings if there are rocks or pieces of glass in and around the water. Don't rely on inflated inner tubes to keep kids afloat, and watch out for overturned air mattresses and rafts in the water. Be sure all the players are good swimmers—unless they plan to stay in the shallow end. There should always be grown-up supervision for all pool, lake, and swimming-hole activities.

Marco Polo is a classic water game that's great fun in a swimming pool or shallow lake. Try the additional variations to make the game even more challenging and exciting.

Ages: 6 and up　　　　　　　　　　　　　　　　　　　　**Players: 2 or more**

Marco Polo

Don't get caught by Marco Polo.

SAFETY

This game is OK for a mixed-age group. If any players are not good swimmers, stay in shallow water. Grown-up supervision is necessary for young children.

How to Play

For the basic game, choose one player to be Marco Polo. That player must close her eyes and count to 10, while the rest of the players scatter throughout the pool. After the count, Marco Polo swims around the pool with her eyes closed until she tags another player. To discover the location of other players, Marco Polo may call out "Marco!" to which the others must answer "Polo!" no matter where they are. When Marco Polo finally tags another player, that player becomes the new Marco Polo.

Variation Play Silent Marco Polo by having all the players remain quiet throughout the game. Marco Polo must listen carefully for sounds or feel the ripples in the water to discover the location of the other players—who could be swimming very close by. Keeping everyone quiet makes the game a little more challenging.

Variation Play Midnight Marco Polo by having all the players close their eyes and keep quiet while being chased by Marco Polo. The suspense mounts as players move around the pool without being able to see one another, until Marco Polo finally bumps into another player. Be prepared for screams and laughs of surprise and delight.

Variation The players are allowed to leave the pool for three seconds at a time, but if Marco Polo happens to say "Fish out of water!" the "fish" is caught and becomes Marco Polo.

2

Here's a high-energy game for two players or two teams. It's great for the shallow end of the pool or lake. The "basket" floats on the surface of the water, so the target is always moving.

Ages: 6 and up

Players: 2 or more

Water Basketball

Sink the ball in the "basket."

Materials

Plastic tub, approximately 2 feet in diameter and 1 to 2 feet tall

Foam, plastic, or Nerf-type ball

For Variations

Foam, plastic, or Nerf-type balls in various colors

Inner tubes, round plastic rings, or air mattresses

SAFETY

This game is recommended for a same-age group. Keep the game in the shallow water, if possible, unless all players are good swimmers. Grown-up supervision is necessary for young children.

How to Play

Find a shallow plastic tub that will float on the surface of the water, hold a foam ball, and not easily tip over. Divide players into two teams, and float the tub in the center of the pool or lake area, with the teams on each side. Play a water variation of basketball, using the tub as the basketball hoop and the foam ball as the basketball. Have one team try to sink the ball into the tub for points, while the other team tries to block and steal the ball, and make their own "basket."

Variation Players take turns shooting the ball from various points in the pool or lake, moving back farther and farther each time they shoot. Suggest that they make some shots backward, with their eyes closed, or with their nondominant hands to make the game more challenging. Keep track of points to see who makes the most baskets. Have each player shoot from a particular spot. When someone makes it, have everyone else take the same shot.

Variation Collect a number of balls in different colors and give one to each player. Have everyone try to ring the basket at the same time and see whose ball remains inside the tub while the others are knocked out.

Variation Players sit on inner tubes, round plastic rings, or air mattresses to make the game more difficult. When players fall off their flotation devices, they may not play again until they are seated.

Here's an underwater diving game that offers several variations. Using "gold nuggets" makes the game more fun, and they're easily spotted under the water.

Gold Diggers

Dive for the "gold."

Materials

10 small stones

Gold waterproof spray paint

Black felt-tipped permanent pen

For Variations

Paint, in various colors

Small objects (see below)

Corks or other objects that float

Wooden match or coin

How to Play

Find 10 small stones, pebbles, or rocks. Turn them into "gold nuggets" by spraying them with gold paint and allowing them to dry. Number each stone using the black felt-tipped permanent pen. Ask everyone to close their eyes and toss the gold nuggets into the pool or shallow lake. On the word "Go!" have the players dive into the water and retrieve as many gold nuggets as they can. The player who collects the most wins. (Note: If one player wears goggles, everyone else should to avoid an unfair advantage.)

Variation Players pick up the nuggets with the highest numbers first, then add up the numbers to find who has the highest score. One player might retrieve more nuggets, but another player may get a higher score after they count the numbers written on the nuggets.

Variation For 10 or fewer players, paint 10 stones a different color for each player. Give the players a set of 10 stones each and have them toss the stones into the pool or lake. Assign a different color to each player and see who can collect all

of his color first. Or paint 10 stones 10 different colors for each player. Have the players retrieve a stone of every color.

Variation Players collect the nuggets with their eyes closed. Or time players individually to see how long it takes each one to retrieve all 10 nuggets. Or see how many nuggets they can collect in one breath.

Variation Toss in a variety of objects for players to collect, such as golf balls, set of keys, cans of soda, weighted plastic rings, metal boxes, action figures, plastic animals, sponges, metallic mirrors (not made of glass), and other things that sink. If you're at the lake, make sure you retrieve everything and leave nothing but water behind when the game is over.

Variation Throw in corks or objects that float. Line the swimmers along the side of the pool or lake, then let them jump in at the same time and retrieve as many of the floating objects as they can.

Variation Throw in one small wooden match (a floater) or a coin (a sinker) and let all the swimmers try to find it.

SAFETY

Make sure all players are good swimmers and that everyone is out of the water before anyone throws stones or other objects into the pool or lake. This game is OK for a mixed-age group. Grown-up supervision is required for young children.

A game of quick thinking with lots of variations. Unfortunately, most of the hands are wet and slippery!

Butterfingers Ball

Catch that ball!

Materials

Diving board or platform

Large plastic balls

For Variations

Inner tube or floating bucket

Large T-shirt

Sun protection lotion or oil

How to Play

As one player jumps off the diving board or platform, another player stands in the shallow end or on the side and throws the ball to the jumper, who tries to catch the ball and hold on to it until she hits the water. Award a point for each time a player manages to hold onto the ball.

Variation Both players hold balls. Leaping off the diving board or platform, the jumper tosses a ball to the player on the side or in the shallow end, while that player tosses his ball to the jumper. Whoever catches a ball gets a point.

Variation Both players hold balls. Leaping off the diving board or platform, the jumper tosses a ball up into the air, while the other player on the side or in the shallow end tries to hit the jumper's ball.

Variation The jumper leaps off the diving board or platform and tries to toss the ball into an inner tube or floating bucket.

Variation In shallow water, players gather in a circle around one player. The player in the middle tosses the ball up in the air and calls out one of the other players' names. That player tries to catch the ball before it hits the water. If the player catches the ball, he goes to the middle. If the player misses, the tosser throws again.

Variation Have a player put on a large T-shirt and slip a large plastic ball under the shirt. The player jumps into the water and tries not to lose the ball. To make it more difficult try it without a T-shirt.

Variation Cover a plastic ball with sun protection lotion or oil. Divide 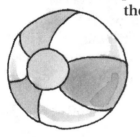 the players into teams, with a team on each side of the pool or lake. Place the ball between the teams. Have the players try to get the ball and carry it back to their side of the pool or lake. It won't be easy when it's all greased up.

SAFETY

Check diving areas for sufficient depth and safety. Make sure all players are good swimmers. This game is OK for a mixed-age group. Grown-up supervision is required for young children.

Another quick-thinking game that creates lots of laughs on the sidelines.

Ages: 6 and up **Players: 2 or more**

Frogman-Jump or Dive!

How quickly can you jump or dive?

Materials

Diving board or platform

How to Play

One player stands on the diving board, platform, or side of the pool or lake at the deep end. Another player calls out "Jump!" or "Dive!" just as the first player leaps into the air. That player must jump or dive, depending on the command. It's fun to watch players try to rearrange their bodies into a jump or dive in midair.

Variation Line up everyone along the edge of the pool or lake at the deep end and have one player tell each of the others whether to jump or dive, one right after another. Those who follow orders correctly are still in the game and get to line up again for another round. Those who don't, sit on the sidelines and watch the fun. Continue to play until only one player is left. That player becomes the one who gives the orders.

Variation Add other commands to the orders, such as "Twist!" "Spiral!" "Frogleg!" "Cannonball!" "Backward!" to make the game more complicated and exciting.

Variation As a player leaps into the air, call out a category, such as "Girls' names!" "Candy bars!" or "Cars!" That player must name something from the category, such as "Rebecca!" if it's girls' names, before hitting the water. Remind players that they can't say the same word twice if a category is called again.

SAFETY

Make sure all players are good swimmers. Don't play in shallow water if the kids are diving as well as jumping. This game is OK for a mixed-age group. Grown-up supervision is required for young children.

Water volleyball is a great way to stay cool in the pool or lake. But it's just the tip of the iceberg when it comes to ball games in the water. Be sure you check out all the variations listed below.

Ages: 8 and up   **Players: 2 or more**

Water Volleyball

Defend your side and score points against your opponents.

Materials

Large plastic ball

Net or rope

For Variations

Tennis ball

Tennis rackets

Inner tube, floating
bucket, or plastic tub

How to Play

Set up a net or use a rope stretched across the pool or shallow part of the lake. Secure the net or rope to trees, or between a couple of hefty chairs on either side of the pool. In a lake, a couple of extra players could hold the rope, float the rope by tying it to Styrofoam floaters, or just use an imaginary line. Divide players into teams. Each team attempts to make the ball land in the water on the other side of the net, while preventing the ball from landing on their side. One point goes to the team who makes the ball land on their opponent's side. At the end of the game, the team with the most points wins.

Variation Keep the game easy for younger kids by having them catch and throw the ball to one another over the net. They gain a point for a catch and lose a point for a miss. Use a giant plastic ball for easier play.

Variation To play Dodge Ball, have the swimmers spread out in the pool or lake. The player with the ball tosses it to tag one of the other players. Players can dodge the ball by swimming away, ducking underwater, or moving side to side. When the player with the ball succeeds in tagging someone, that player becomes "IT." Play the game blindfolded for added excitement. Or have the players remain "stuck" to their spots while the ball is thrown at them from a distance. For a change, use sponges instead of a ball. Or line up the kids along the edge of the pool or lake and have one player remain in the pool,

Play in the shallow end or be sure all players are good swimmers. This game is OK for a mixed-age group. Ask players not to throw the ball too hard, or at another player's face.

closing her eyes and holding the ball. When a player is tagged, that player falls into the pool. Continue until all the players are wet.

Variation To play Tennis, set up a net and hit a tennis ball back and forth with a tennis racket. The player who lets the ball hit the water loses a point. Or have all players with rackets try to hit the tennis ball into an inner tube, floating basket, or plastic tub. Keep track of points.

Here's an underwater obstacle course where kids are divers looking for lost treasure on a sunken ship.

Shipwreck

Make it through a shipwreck obstacle course, bringing back the sunken treasure.

Materials

Objects to swim around, through, and under (see below) that are weighted with sand-filled plastic bottles

Inexpensive costume jewelry, gold-painted stones, or small plastic toys

For Variations

Rubber sharks or sponges

Broomstick or pole

How to Play

Set up an obstacle course under the water with a variety of objects, such as hula hoops, plastic chairs, large rings, and ropes, weighted and arranged so players can swim underneath them. Disperse costume jewelry, painted stones, and plastic toys throughout. When you have created your "sunken ship," have divers swim through, around, and underneath the obstacles, and retrieve the "treasure."

Variation Have the first diver chart out a course through the obstacles. The rest of the players follow the leader exactly through the sunken ship. Players who forget the path are "out of the water."

Variation Keep the course challenging by changing it from time to time. Or have the players do the course with their eyes closed.

11

SAFETY

Grown-up supervision is necessary. This game is OK for a mixed-age group. Make sure all obstacles can be freed quickly if someone gets stuck.

Variation Toss in a few rubber sharks for the divers to avoid while retrieving the sunken treasure. Or use the rubber sharks to create an obstacle course on top of the water. Have the players swim around the sharks to reach the other side of the pool. The one who swims through the course the fastest without touching the sharks is the winner. Use sponges instead of sharks, if you prefer.

Here are a few active, competitive games to burn off energy in the water.

Water Relays

Beat the other team in a race to the other side.

Materials

2 Ping-Pong balls

2 tennis balls

2 balloons

2 plastic inflatable rafts

Hula hoops

How to Play

PING-PONG BALL RACE Divide each team in half and have one half stand on one side of the pool and the other half stand on the other side of the pool. On one side of the pool place Ping-Pong balls in front of each team. When you say "Go!" the first players on each team begin blowing the ball to the other side where the other half of their teams are waiting. When the ball reaches the other side, have another player take over, and blow the ball back to the starting line. Repeat laps until all players have had a turn. The first team to complete the race wins.

TENNIS BALL RACE Place tennis balls in the water in front of the teams. The first players must push the balls across the pool with their chins.

BALLOON RACE The players use their noses to push balloons across the pool.

RAFT RACE A player from each team paddles a plastic raft across the pool and back, lying on his stomach. The second group races across and back lying on their backs. The third group sits on the raft and uses only their feet to kick the raft across the pool and back. The fourth group pushes the third group across the pool and back on the raft. The fifth group races with their eyes closed. Try the game with two players on a raft, then add another, and another, until the raft sinks. Continue to make up different ways of getting across the pool until a team wins, or everyone is worn out.

SAFETY

All players should be good swimmers. These games are recommended for a same-age group. Adult supervision is recommended.

KANGAROO RACE Have teams line up along one end of the pool or lake and have them jump to the other side. They should always be able to touch the bottom with their feet. As the players jump, they will get slower and slower and more awkward, which makes it more challenging. Have the second team members walk, the third team members run, and fourth team members go backward, and so on.

HOOP RACE Toss several hula hoops onto the water. Have the players dive in, swim to the hoops, slip them over their bodies, and continue collecting more hoops.

It's easy to get wet when there's a pool or lake nearby.
But is it possible to keep something dry? Find out.

Keep It Dry

Try to keep something dry while everything else gets wet.

Materials

Stones, cotton balls, or marshmallows

For Variations

Old clothes: gloves, hats, pants, shirts, and socks

Large bath towels

SAFETY

All players should be good swimmers. This game is OK for a mixed-age group. Adult supervision is recommended.

How to Play

Give each player a small object that changes when it gets wet to hold in one hand, such as a stone, cotton ball, or marshmallow. Players should swim from one end of the pool or lake to the other, holding the object and trying to keep it dry. The swimmer with the driest object wins.

Variation Players swim with objects in both hands or on top of their heads, on a spoon in their mouths, or set on the backs of their hands.

Variation Wearing different articles of clothing, the players swim across the pool trying to keep the clothing dry. Begin with the hats, which should be fairly easy. Add gloves and have the swimmers try to keep them dry while swimming a lap. For subsequent laps, swimmers wear shirts, socks, and then pants.

Variation Have a relay race where players exchange a large bath towel. Divide players into teams and have the first players on each team swim from one side of the pool or lake to the other, holding the towel up to keep it dry. Repeat the laps with all team players and see which team has the driest towel at the end of the race.

*Here's a variation on an old favorite,
this time played wet instead of dry.*

Duck, Duck, Shark!

Get to safety before getting tagged.

Materials

Sponges, 1 for each player

For Variations

Large plastic ball

How to Play

Place a sponge in the back of each kid's bathing suit so it sticks out enough to be grabbed. The kids should make a circle in the shallow end of the pool or lake, and choose one player to be the Shark. The Shark swims slowly and menacingly around the outside of the circle, while the others, like sitting ducks, wait for the Shark to attack. When the Shark grabs a sponge from the back of a player's bathing suit, the Duck chases the Shark around the outside of the circle. If the Duck tags the Shark, the Shark must remain a Shark for another play. If the Shark makes it back to the open space before being tagged by the Duck, the Duck loses and becomes the Shark.

Variation To play Octopus, have the players form a circle, each holding onto the next player's foot with one hand. Toss a ball into the center of the circle, and have the players try to grab the ball with their free hands. Whoever gets the ball steps out of the circle and the play continues until there is only one player left.

Variation To play Torpedo, have the group form a circle around a player who's "IT" in the middle. One player throws the ball to IT. As the player tries to catch the ball, all the other players swim as far away as possible. When the player catches the ball, she calls out "Freeze!" and the group of swimmers must stay where they are. The player with the ball tries to hit one of the scattered swimmers without moving around the pool or lake. If the thrower misses, everyone swims away again until she retrieves the ball and yells "Freeze!" If someone is hit, that person becomes IT.

A game of skill with a couple of variations.

Save Our Ship

Toss a "lifeboat" to the "sinking ship" and save the day.

Materials

3 wood blocks (approximately 4 inches square), plastic containers with lids, or half-gallon milk cartons folded and taped into blocks

3 plastic or Styrofoam rings or plastic inner tubes

String or rope

SAFETY

Remind the rescuers to toss the rings at the feet, not at the face or head. This game is recommended for a same-age group. Adult supervision is recommended.

How to Play

Float the wood blocks, plastic containers, or milk carton blocks in the water. Cut three long pieces of string or rope. Tie string or rope to each of the rings or inner tubes. Have each player toss the rings over the floating objects in order to "rescue" them, then pull them ashore using the string or rope.

Variation Give each player a certain number of tries to ring the floaters. Or give them points for a first attempt, a second attempt, and so on. Or time the players, giving them one to two minutes to accomplish the rescue.

Variation Have a person float on the water. Rescuers toss rings around his foot and pull him to shore.

17

An exciting and scary game with Jaws nipping at the swimmers' heels.

Ages: 6 and up

Players: 5 or more

Jaws

Escape from Jaws!

For Variations

Sponge, ball, or other floating object

How to Play

Gather the group together and form a circle. Select one player to be Jaws and move outside of the circle. Select another to be Fishfood and move into the center of the circle. Have the remaining players hold hands to keep the circle intact. Jaws must circle around the outside and try to get inside to tag Fishfood. Jaws can try to swim underneath the players' hands or figure out another way to get inside the circle, but cannot break any hands apart. The players in the circle, meanwhile, try to keep Jaws out. Fishfood can tease Jaws by moving in and out of the circle, but he must be careful not to get caught. When Jaws finally gets his snack, Fishfood becomes Jaws and a new player is selected to play Fishfood.

Variation Instead of using Jaws as the menace, try Toxic Waste. A sponge, ball, or other floating object becomes Toxic Waste and is placed in the center of the circle of players who are holding hands. The players then try to pull a player into contact with Toxic Waste. Anyone touched by Toxic Waste leaves the circle and the game continues.

Variation Play Sharks and Minnows by selecting one person to be the Shark, while the others are Minnows. The Shark waits at the deep end with her eyes closed, while the Minnows line up at the shallow end. When the Shark yells "Feed Me!" the Minnows try to swim to the other end without getting caught by the Shark, whose eyes remain closed throughout the game. If the Shark tags a Minnow, the Minnow becomes a Shark, too. Minnows that reach the deep end without getting caught must turn around and swim back to the shallow end to become free. It gets trickier as more and more Minnows become Sharks. Minnows must always go forward, but Sharks can go any direction, as long as their eyes are closed.

SAFETY

This is an active game, so be sure all players have stamina and are good swimmers. This game is OK for a mixed-age group. Adult supervision is recommended.

CHAPTER TWO

OCEAN & BEACH

Take the kids to the ocean and enjoy some sunny fun at the beach. The sand and water offer many opportunities for good times—why not build a sand castle or ride the surf? Or you can go on a Dino Dig, play Follow the Pirate, set up a beach party, or create a sandpainting. At the beach, you can make crafts, play sand games, and learn about the many parts of ocean life.

But while you're there, keep the fun long-lasting by bringing along the essentials—lots of drinks and snacks, extra towels and sunglasses, and plenty of sun protection lotion.

These pitching cups, also called cestas, can be used in the sand, water, or air and are great for the beach.

Ages: 6 and up

Players: 2 or more

Jai Alai

Play catch with your own pitching cups.

Materials

Plastic gallon milk or bleach jugs, 1 per person

Felt-tipped permanent pen

Scissors

Electrical tape

Tennis ball

What to Do

First, thoroughly clean the milk or bleach jugs. Draw a cutting line, using a felt-tipped pen to trace a scoop-shaped cup. Cut along the line with scissors, keeping edges as smooth as possible. If kids are doing the cutting, they will need grown-up help. Cover over any sharp edges with electrical tape for safety. Now it's time to use your jai alai cups for fun at the beach.

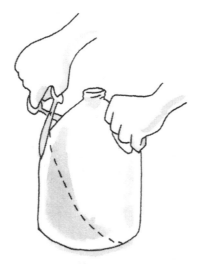

How to Play

Players should stand a few feet apart from each other. Place a tennis ball in one of the scoops. Using the scoop, the first player tosses the ball to another player, who catches the ball with the scoop. No hands allowed! Two players can toss the ball back and forth, or three players can toss it around in a circle. Or toss it randomly to members of the group. Stand farther and farther apart to make the game more challenging.

Variation Use the scoops to dig in the sand and create sand castles or make creative designs. You can also dig for sand crabs or other beach life, or carry sand from one area to another. And you can use them as molds to make large bricks for a fortress.

Variation The scoops make great splashing toys. Just scoop up a bunch of water and hurl it at your opponent. Or use the scoops to bail out a raft or sand-castle moat. Use the scoops as paddles for a raft, too.

SAFETY

Be careful not to swing the scoops with sand inside, or someone might get hurt. Cover all sharp plastic edges with electrical tape.

A great toy to use at the ocean, lake, river, or pond where there are lots of interesting things to look at under the water. You might even try it in the swimming pool or bathtub.

Ages: 5 and up

Players: 1 or more

Sea Scope

See underwater life.

Materials

Half-gallon milk carton

Plastic wrap

Waterproof glue

Clear tape

For Variations

2 plastic tubes

Piece of clear, hard plastic

✚ SAFETY

Watch the kids as they walk with the sea scope. Remind them to look up once in a while to see if there are obstacles or dangers ahead.

What to Do

Thoroughly clean and dry the half-gallon milk carton. Cut a circle out of the bottom of the milk carton. To make the lens, stretch plastic wrap tightly over the bottom of the carton. Attach the plastic wrap to the jug's sides by gluing it to one side and taping it securely, repeat with the opposite side. Repeat the procedure with the last two sides, smoothing the wrap as you go to get a clear lens. Open the spout of the milk carton, place the lens in the water, and peer into the water.

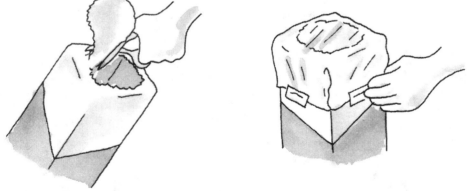

Variation Use two plastic tubes taped together to make underwater binoculars, or use one long plastic tube to make an underwater telescope.

Variation Use a small piece of clear, hard plastic instead of plastic wrap to make the sea scope sturdier and longer lasting.

24

*The fun comes with the first splash of ice water. It'll
be refreshing on the hottest days of summer!*

Ages: 6 and up

Players: 4 or more

Ice-Water Relay

Don't spill the ice water on yourself!

Materials

2 flat pans

Ice water and cubes

For Variations

Sand crabs or large crabs

Objects to fill the pan (see below)

SAFETY

Don't fill the pan with sand since it might get into the players' eyes.

How to Play

Divide players into two teams and have them line up along the beach so that the surf laps their feet. Give the players at the front of each line a pan of ice water and cubes. The players must pass the pan over their heads from one person to the next, along the line, until the pan reaches the end of the line. At the end, the last player runs with the pan back up to the front of the line, and the pan is passed back again, until all players have a chance to run the pan to the front of the line. If the pan spills and there is no more ice water in the pan, the player who has the pan must run to the ice cooler and refill the pan with ice water, then return to the line and continue the play. Watch the fun as the ice-cold water splashes down on the players!

Variation Playing in the surf makes the action slow down a little, adding to the excitement and challenge. If you want a vigorous game, play on the sand or in deeper water.

Variation Add other objects to the pan to make it interesting, such as fruit-flavored drink, popcorn, feathers, cotton balls, gold coins, potato chips, peanuts, and so on. Count up the total contents at the end of the game to see which team lost the most items. And be sure to clean up after the game is over.

Gather the kids together, add water, sand, and sunshine, and you've got a beach party!

Ages: 6 and up

Players: 4 or more

Have fun at the beach.

Materials

Bathing suits

Towels

Sun protection lotion

Beach games to play

Sand toys and squirt guns

Rafts and inner tubes

Hibachi or barbecue grill

Food for a cookout

For Variations

Beach movie

What to Do

Gather the kids, bathing suits, towels, sun protection lotion, and beach stuff, including toys and items for a cookout, and head for your favorite ocean. Play group games, such as beach volleyball, Frisbee, or jai alai. Build a sand castle, have a squirt-gun fight, float on rafts and inner tubes, and play some of the games suggested in this book. When everyone's had enough, light up the hibachi or barbecue grill and roast hot dogs or hamburgers.

Variation If the weather turns bad, take the beach party home. Have guests wear bathing suits, spread out towels, eat beach snacks, and spend the day watching a beach movie or doing some of the indoor water activities, such as making Frozen Slushies, Ocean Wave Bottles, or Water Art.

SAFETY

Be sure to cover everyone adequately with sun protection lotion and repeat applications often, especially if the kids are spending a lot of time in the water. Watch the kids closely as they play in the water. Give them rules about how far out they can go and how long they can stay in the water.

Sand is such a versatile play material—there is an endless number of things you can do with it! All you need are some creative ideas and some gadgets to help you construct your sand castles and sea shapes.

Ages: 5 and up
Players: 1 or more

Sand Castles & Sea Shapes

Make structures and shapes from sand.

Materials

Action figures, plastic animals and dinosaurs, fake fish

Things to dig: ladles, shovels, spades, and spoons

Things to draw: combs, forks, knives, pencils, Popsicle sticks, rakes, toothpicks, and wide-toothed brushes

What to Do

Gather as many objects as you can find to take with you to the beach or sandbox. You can pick up some of these items at thrift stores or on sale at drug and grocery stores. Find a sandy spot and let the kids go to work.

Things to Create

Sand castles with moats filled with water and fake floating fish. Make dribble castles by piling up a mound of sand, then scooping very wet sand up in handfuls and letting it dribble over the top of the mound. Looks creepy, weird, and unusual.

Small-scale communities, complete with sand crabs, action figures, or plastic animals and dinosaurs.

Self-portraits or portraits of your friends using damp sand to draw.

Buried-alive victims, covered from neck to foot with sand. Reshape a body next to the head from sand to create a super

Things to move: bowls, boxes, cups, dishes, margarine tubs, measuring cups, pails, and plastic jars

Things to shape: flowerpots, gelatin molds, milk carton, paper towel tube, Playdoh accessories, springform pans, and unusually shaped containers

Other tools: basters, colanders, cookie cutters, dough crumblers, funnels, potato mashers, rotary hand mixers, salt and pepper shakers, sieves, and sifters

SAFETY

Make sure the kids don't bury anyone's face in the sand. Buried-alive victims' faces should be protected from flying sand.

hero, animal, or monster with a real head. (A fun photo trick: Bury a friend in the sand from the neck down. Have another friend stand over the friend with his back to the camera; the buried friend should face the camera. Have your standing friend bend over so that his head won't show in the picture and pretend to lift your buried friend's head out of the sand by grasping both sides of her head. In the picture he will look headless, and as if he's picking his head out of the sand!)

Molded shapes, using some of the objects you brought along. Create sand reproductions of your favorite gelatin salad or other interesting shapes. Use the funnel to shape a spaceship, a milk carton to mold a skyscraper, or a paper towel tube to create a tunnel.

Canals, water shoots, and waterfalls in a mountain of damp sand. First, make a sand mountain. Then, carve out tunnels, shoots, ditches, and rivers down the mountain and around the bottom to create a lake. Slowly pour water at the top of the mountain and watch it spiral, twist, and turn down the slope. Add small boats to the water trip.

Your own game board, using wet sand as a foundation. Smooth the wet sand first, then use your finger or a Popsicle stick to carve out squares for checkers, chess, coin toss, bingo, or any other game you can think of. Use shells as markers.

Other ideas: an Egyptian pyramid, a small car, a dinosaur skeleton that's just been discovered, a rat maze, a plate of fake food, a school of fish, your name in 3-D, a set of fossils, monsters, snakes, crabs, alligators, and mysterious treasure maps.

Add finishing touches to your sand art using driftwood, feathers, fish bones, pinecones, seaweed, shells, smooth stones, sticks and twigs, and other items found on the beach.

Digging for dinosaur bones is a perfect project for the beach.
You can never tell when a T-rex might turn up.

Dino Dig

Discover buried dinosaurs at the beach.

Materials

Small plastic dinosaurs

For Variations

Pipe cleaners or Popsicle sticks

String or glue

Spoons and small paint brushes

Plastic eggs

Saucepan

Cornstarch

Powdered alum (optional, available at drug stores)

What to Do

Mark off an area of the beach with a stick. While the kids are off playing, bury a number of plastic dinosaurs in the sand. Put some of them near the wet shore, some in the surf, and some in the dry sand. Have the kids go on a dinosaur hunt to find all the hidden dinosaurs. Watch for any that may float out to sea if the surf uncovers them.

Variation Create a dinosaur skeleton using pipe cleaners or Popsicle sticks. Tie or glue them together before you go to the beach, then bury the skeleton in the sand when you get there. Show the kids how to carefully dig up the bones, using spoons and brushes. Have them create their own dinosaur skeletons using pipe cleaners and Popsicle sticks to make spines, ribs, legs, feet, and other parts. Award prizes for most creative, scary, and so on.

Variation Fill plastic eggs with plastic dinosaurs and bury the eggs in the sand. Let the kids discover them.

Variation This takes a little work but it's well worth it. In a saucepan, mix 2 cups of sand with 1 cup of cornstarch, 1 tablespoon of powdered alum (it'll help the mixture hold its shape), and ¾ cup water. Cook and stir on low heat until mixture is thick. Cool until lukewarm. Use your hands or plastic egg molds to shape the sand mixture into egg shapes around small plastic dinosaurs. Allow to dry overnight or a couple of days. Handle the egg shapes carefully, and place them in the sand. Let the kids discover the eggs, break them open, and find the surprise inside.

The beach is the perfect place to cast your mark in sand. Here are several ways you can turn the beach into your sand canvas.

Sand-Casting

Make molded shapes in the sand.

Materials

Sand

Water

Plaster of paris

Bucket, bowl, or coffee can

Glue

Little objects to decorate the casting (see below)

What to Do

Moisten the sand with water, smooth it with your hands, and make a wall of sand to shape the design. Make an imprint with a mold, a can, your foot or hand, some small toys, a large shell, or anything you wish. Mix up a batch of plaster of paris in a bucket, bowl, or coffee can according to the package directions. Fill the print with the plaster and let it set, about 15 minutes. Brush away the sand and admire your new casting. When it has fully dried overnight,

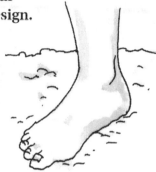

31

SAFETY

Grown-ups should supervise activities with the plaster of paris.

paint the casting and glue on objects, such as feathers, shells, seaweed, and small toy animals, boats, and cars, to make it unique and decorative.

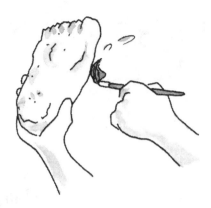

Variation Cast an animal track by locating bird or animal footprints at the beach. You can usually find them early in the morning, in the wet part of a sandy beach. Fill the track with plaster of paris, let set, and pick it up carefully, brushing away excess sand. Do your own footprint as well.

Variation Write your name backward in the sand in 3-D letters, and fill with plaster. Or make giant monster feet, a mysterious footpath leading to buried treasure, or a sand sculpture with collectibles from the beach.

Variation Make a face by carving a round circle, pushing in eyes or using shells for eyes and other facial details, then pour in plaster.

You can make your sandpainting in several ways by using these techniques. Or experiment and make your own colors and designs.

Sandpainting

Make colorful sandpaintings.

Materials

Sand

Colored chalk

For Variations

Large sheet of paper

Salt

Medium-size glass jar

Food coloring or poster paint

Small baby food jar

Toothpick

White glue

✚ SAFETY

The kids will think the sand looks good enough to eat, but tell them not to put it in their mouths. It still tastes like sand! Be careful when using the glass jar for the sandscape.

What to Do

Put some dry sand in a number of bowls. "Color" each bowl of sand with a different colored chalk by simply rubbing it back and forth over the sand. The rough sand will cause the colored chalk to sift into the sand, and tint it. Use a folded sheet of paper to hold the colored sand, and pour slowly onto a smooth sand surface to make your design.

Variation Paint white glue on a large sheet of paper and lightly pour colored sand over the glue. Pour off the sand that doesn't stick. Repeat with various colors until a unique design appears. Make a picture of an animal, a free-form shape, or a stained glass window.

Variation Squirt white glue in thin lines on paper, or write your name, then pour colored sand over the glue lines. Remove excess sand and repeat with other colors.

Variation Use different colors of regular sand instead of coloring the sand. Contrast dark and light to make a natural picture.

Variation You can use salt instead of sand, if you prefer. Or you can use food coloring with wet sand, by stirring the wet sand around in a jar and adding food coloring. Or you can add poster paint to the sand, shake it up in a jar, and watch it turn colors.

Variation Use the colored sand to make a "sandscape." Find a small baby food jar and clean it out thoroughly. When it's dry, fill it with ½ inch of one color of sand. Repeat with other colors of sand. Stick a toothpick between the sand and the inside of the jar and make a design. Fill the jar completely with sand and attach the lid. Don't shake the jar!

You can make these sand candles right on the beach, then bring them home and display them on the mantel.

Ages: 8 and up

Sand Candles

Players: 2 or more

Make beautiful sand candles.

Materials

String

Short stick

Ball of modeling clay

Old crayons or candle stubs

Large cooking pot or coffee can

Hibachi

Pot holders

For Variations

Small objects (see below)

Sandpaper

Paint

What to Do

Tie string in the middle of a stick so that it hangs 4 inches long, and attach a clay ball at the end to weigh it down. Dig a 4-by-4-inch hole (or any size you prefer) in the sand. Place the stick across the hole with the string dangling down the middle. Peel crayons of similar colors and place them and old candle stubs in a large cooking pot or coffee can. Melt the crayons over the hibachi, with grown-up supervision. Using pot holders, remove the pot or can from heat and pour wax carefully into the sand hole. Let wax cool for several hours, then dig out the candle, brush off excess sand, and admire your work.

Variation Make different shapes in the sand and pour in the wax. You might try a hand shape, either flat or sticking straight into the sand, or push a toy animal into the sand to create an animal-shaped candle. Then fill with wax.

34

SAFETY

Working with hot wax or hot sand requires grown-up supervision. Work one-on-one, use caution, and work slowly.

Variation Add small objects like broken bottle bits, empty crab shells, seashells, seaweed, and other beach items to your candles to make them more interesting.

Ahoy, matey! You've been shipwrecked on this deserted island and you've got to watch yer step. Pirates have set up booby traps and other dangers, so keep a lookout as you make your way around Pirates' Cove.

Ages: 6 and up

Players: 2 or more

Follow the Pirate

Navigate yourself through the pirates' obstacle course.

Materials

Discarded items from the sea (see below)

Digging tools

For Variations

Gold coins filled with chocolate or some other treasures

Large stick

SAFETY Make sure the obstacle course is in a safe place.

What to Do

Set up an obstacle course right on the beach using items found around you, such as pieces of wood, seaweed, old rope, and other discarded items from the sea. Use digging tools to make a trench that the kids can walk through, over, and around. Make the trenches narrow, deep, and twisting every which way so they're not easy to navigate. Next, make a series of hurdles to leap over or crawl under, using sand mounds, sticks, and pieces of wood. Make the hurdles narrow and tall. Use the seaweed to create a maze to follow; if you can't find seaweed, use rope or draw out a maze using a long stick dragged in the sand. Make some footprints for the kids to step in and follow. Make the footprints small, large, close together, far apart, forward, backward, sideways, and with only one foot. Then tell the kids to follow the pirates' path carefully. They can't fall off or the alligators will get them—if the quicksand doesn't.

Variation Have the obstacle course lead to some buried treasure— gold coins filled with chocolate or other pirate bounty.

Variation After they've conquered the course, have the kids follow it backward or blindfolded.

Variation Create a version of beach hopscotch, marking out the grid with a large stick in the wet sand.

CHAPTER THREE

The kids don't need a great big pool to have fun in the water. Kids of all ages will enjoy activities for the backyard kiddie pool. You'd be surprised how even teenagers like to get goofy and fool around in the kiddie pool—as long as nobody's looking! Very little setup is necessary, just assemble your plastic pool, set it on the lawn for a soft landing, and add water and kids. While the kids are in the pool, introduce them to games like Splash Machine, Shark Bait, Frog Invasion, and Gone Fishing, for an afternoon of frolicking fun in the water.

*Here's a great way to get wet on a hot day, and
fill the kids' wading pool at the same time.*

Splash Machine

Use teamwork to fill the pool.

Materials

Bucket or pail

For Variations

Stopwatch

Buckets, 1 for each player

Large sponges, 1 for each player

Variety of objects that hold water (see below), 1 for each player

SAFETY

Make sure all the players know they're bound to get wet. Don't use containers with sharp edges—someone could get cut.

How to Play

Line the kids up from the water spigot to the wading pool. Give the player nearest the spigot a bucket or pail. Have him fill the pail with water and pass it to the next person in line, who will pass it to the next, and so on, until the pail of water reaches the end of the line. The last person dumps the water—what's left of it—into the pool, then runs to the spigot and starts the process again.

Variaton To make the game more fun, use a stopwatch and have the kids pass the bucket faster and faster down the line each time they play. They'll be lucky if there's any water left at all to pour into the kiddie pool by the end of the game.

Variaton Give everyone a bucket. This really keeps the line moving and causes all kinds of spills, splashes, and laughs.

Variaton Give everyone large soaked sponges instead of buckets and watch the water fly everywhere but into the kiddie pool.

Variaton Use a variety of containers to pass the water, instead of only buckets. Give all the players a chance to use each container by having everyone pass them down the line, one right after the other. You might use large cans, ice cube trays, baking pans, plastic coffee cups, sponges, old plastic purses, or dog dishes—anything that will hold water.

*Watch out! The Shark looks awfully hungry—
and you just might be the bait.*

Shark Bait

Pass the ball back and forth without letting the Shark catch it.

Materials

Medium-size plastic ball

For Variations

Small plastic balls, 1 for each player

How to Play

Have everyone sit in a circle around the inside edge of the kiddie pool. Have one player be the Shark and sit in the middle of the circle. Give the ball to someone in the circle to toss back and forth between all the players without letting the Shark intercept and catch it. When the Shark finally catches the ball, the one who threw it trades places with the Shark and becomes the new Shark.

Variation Give all the players a small plastic ball and let them toss the balls all at the same time. Then watch as everyone, including the Shark, scrambles for a ball.

Variation Have the Shark close her eyes while the ball is tossed, so it's more difficult for her to catch the ball. Or have the players in the circle close their eyes, while the Shark watches for the ball. Use a light, soft ball so kids don't get hurt while their eyes are closed.

SAFETY

Tell the kids to toss the ball up high so no one gets hit in the face.

A great game for little kids that's just right for the kiddie pool.

Ages: 5 to 9

Players: 2 or more

Buried Treasure

Find the buried treasure at the bottom of the sea.

Materials

Pennies

For Variations

Variety of small items (see below)

How to Play

Collect a bunch of pennies from a piggy bank. Have the kids stand outside the pool with their backs to the pool, while you toss in all the pennies. On the word "Go!" have the kids turn around, jump into the pool, and scramble for the coins.

Variation Have them scramble for the coins with their eyes closed.

Variation Have them take turns collecting the pennies and time them as they go. See who finds all of them the fastest.

Variation Use a variety of search items, such as unpopped popcorn kernels, marbles, small pebbles, fake pearls, and beads.

SAFETY

Make sure the younger kids do not put the small items in their mouths.

40

Make your own frogs and watch them "hop" into the water.

Frog Invasion

See who has the most talented jumping frog.

Materials

Small, smooth stones, 5 for each player

Green non–water-soluble paint

Black felt-tipped permanent pens

Plastic shower curtain (optional)

How to Play

Find five small, smooth stones for each player and paint them green with non–water-soluble paint. Allow to dry. Draw a grid with a black felt-tipped pen on the bottom of the kiddie pool by either drawing concentric circles, parallel lines, or random circles. (If you don't want to write on the pool itself, write on an old plastic shower curtain. Then lay it on the inside of the pool and cover it with water.) Label the space in the circles or lines with point values. For example, if you've drawn

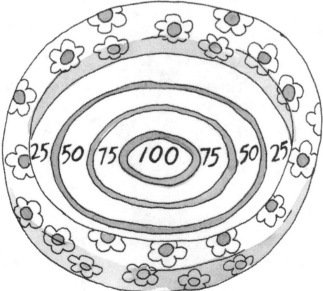

five concentric circles, label the inside circle with 100, the next circle with 75, the next with 50, the next with 25, and the last outer circle with 10. If you're using lines, label the farthest space 100, the next 75, and so on, with the closest space being 10. When the stones are dry, let the kids personalize them by drawing funny frog faces on the stones using the black felt-tipped permanent pen. You might suggest that they give their frogs names, too, to tell them apart. Have the kids stand some distance from the pool and "hop" their frogs into the pool. Add up points to see who's got the most talented frog.

Variation Play a game of Frog Toss by having one player toss his frog into the pool. The next player tries to hit that frog with her frog. If she hits it, she gets to keep the frog. If not, she leaves her frog in the pool with the other frog and the next player tries his luck. The player with the most frogs at the end of the game wins.

Variation Instead of putting points into the pool grid, write a silly task. When a frog lands in that circle, have the player follow the instructions inside. You might include tasks such as "Splash yourself," "Blow bubbles in the pool," "Make wet footprints," "Wet your hair," "Hop on one foot in the pool," or "Do the backstroke in the kiddie pool."

Make your own Niña, Pinta, and Santa Maria
to sail the kiddie-pool ocean.

Walnut Ships

Sail your walnut ship at sea.

Materials

Walnuts, unshelled

Nutcracker

Clay or Playdoh

Scissors

Paper

Tape

Toothpicks

For Variations

Half-gallon milk carton

Spray paint and decals

Stapler

Balloon

Styrofoam containers or other materials that float (see below)

What to Do

Crack the walnuts in half and remove the insides. (Eat them, if you like.) Fill the hollow shells with clay or Playdoh. Use scissors to cut out small flags from paper, approximately 1 inch square, and decorate them anyway you want—with your country flag, a pirate insignia, or your name and unique flag design. Tape the paper to the toothpick top, or insert the toothpick into the paper to make a sail. Stick the other end of the toothpick into the clay. Set the ship to sail in the kiddie pool.

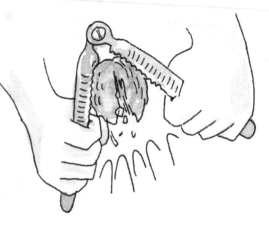

Tell the kids to be careful with the toothpicks. If you are concerned about the sharp ends, break them off.

How to Play

Place two ships in the water at one end of the pool and motion your hand in the water to make the ships move forward. Have a race to see whose ship can reach the other side of the pool first.

Variation **Place the ships in the water and then start an ocean storm by rocking the water with your hands or body. The first one to tip over is the loser.**

Variation Drop ships into the water from a distance to see which ones land right side up and which ones turn over.

Variation Make a large ship from a milk carton by cutting out one side of the carton, painting the carton with spray paint, and adding a few decals.

Variation Cut one side off a milk carton and staple the spout nearly closed, leaving a small opening in the middle. Inflate a balloon but do not tie it off. While holding the end carefully, place it in the carton with the end stuck through the opening in the spout. Place the milk carton boat in the kiddie pool and let go. Watch the boat go as the air seeps out of the balloon.

Variation Styrofoam containers make good boats, and so do pieces of driftwood, margarine containers, and small plastic boxes.

Ages: 6 and up

Players: 2 or more

Pop the Piranha

Be the first to "pop your piranha."

Materials

Balloons

Black felt-tipped permanent pen

How to Play

Inflate the balloons and tie them off. Using the black felt-tipped permanent pens, have the kids draw a fish face on the front to look like menacing piranhas, with big mean eyes, open mouths, and lots of sharp, jagged teeth. Toss a balloon for each player into the kiddie pool. On the word "Go!" have the kids jump into the pool, grab a balloon, and try to pop it by sitting on it. The water makes everything slippery, so there will be a lot of falling and getting wet. Whoever pops a balloon first, wins.

Variation Fill the pool with balloons and let the kids pop as many as they can. Whoever pops the most, wins.

Variation Play balloon volleyball in the kiddie pool by batting the piranha balloon back and forth. Tell kids not to let the mouth part hit their hands so they won't get bitten!

Variation Fill a balloon with water. Have the kids sit in a circle in the pool while one

45

SAFETY

Tell the kids not to pop the balloons with their mouths, only their hands or bottoms. If they have trouble squeezing the balloons to make them pop, let them use a toothpick, under grown-up supervision.

player walks around the outside of the circle with the water balloon. Have her try to pop the balloon by squeezing it with her hands over each kid's head as she walks around, until it finally bursts. The player who gets wet chases the balloon popper around the pool and tries to tag her. If he does, he gets to go back to the circle. If he doesn't, he has to be the balloon popper.

A musical game in the water, where kids play like frogs.

Frogs on a Lily Pad

Find a place on a "lily pad."

Materials

Musical instrument (a harmonica, triangle, kazoo, or bells)

Green plastic garbage bags

How to Play

Find a musical instrument that you can play outdoors (without electricity). Cut out giant, round "lily pads" about the size of a medium pizza from green plastic garbage bags. Float the lily pads on the water and have the kids stand around the outside of the kiddie pool. Tell the "frogs" you are going to play your musical instrument and when you stop, they must jump into the pool, find a lily pad, and sit down on it. After a practice run, remove one lily pad so you have just enough for all the kids but one. Play the instrument for a minute or so, then stop playing. When the music stops, the kids scramble for lily pads to sit on. The one left without a lily pad is "out" until the game is over.

Variation Instead of lily pads, make "boats," "icebergs," "magic carpets," or anything you want. Then have the kids act appropriately by jumping on the ship, leaping onto the iceberg, or landing on the magic carpet.

SAFETY

The pool is slippery, so don't let the kids get too wild. Be sure the pool is on a soft surface so when they fall or sit down they won't get hurt.

Let the kids keep the goldfish after the fun is over.

Gone Fishing

Catch a fish!

Materials

Goldfish, at least 1 for each player

Small nets, 1 for each player

Tap water conditioner

Small plastic jars or plastic sandwich bags

For Variations

Plastic windup fish

Styrofoam containers

Food strainer

Masking tape

SAFETY

Instruct the kids on how to treat the goldfish, and tell them how to care for the fish when they get home.

How to Play

Purchase some inexpensive goldfish at the pet store, along with a small net for each player. Fill the kiddie pool with water and add tap water conditioner, according to package instructions. Release the goldfish into the kiddie pool. Let the kids fish for their own goldfish using the nets—not an easy task! Write the kids' names in black felt-tipped permanent pen on small plastic jars or plastic sandwich bags, fill the containers with water treated with tap water conditioner, and give the containers to the kids to hold their catch and carry these new pets home.

Variation Buy some plastic windup fish at a toy store and place them in the pool. Then have the kids race to capture as many plastic fish as they can.

Variation Cut out fish shapes from Styrofoam containers and float them in the pool. Let the kids try to catch as many as they can with a food strainer, or tape their fingers closed with masking tape and let them use their hands.

A twist on the tug-of-war game,
where you try not to get wet.

Don't Get Wet!

Pull the other team into the kiddie pool with the rope.

Materials

Long rope

For Variations

Blindfolds, 1 for each player

Garden hose

Food coloring or plastic alligators

SAFETY

Be careful of rope burn. You can have the kids wear gloves to protect their hands if they're using rope. Stop the game if any kids fall down so they don't get trampled.

How to Play

Divide the players into two teams with equal numbers on each team. Place a long length of rope across the kiddie pool, leaving equal amounts of rope on each side. Have each team stand on either side of the pool and hold the rope. On the word "Go!" each team must try to pull the other team into the pool. The first team to get wet—or let go of the rope—loses.

Variation Use a garden hose. It's hard to hold on to, which can add to the fun, and it's less likely to give the kids rope burn.

Variation Have players compete one-on-one. They should stand across the pool from each other, just outside the rim. Give each one an end of rope and tell them to try to tug the other player into the water without moving their feet. Eventually one player will lose his balance and fall in.

Variation Tell the kids that the pool is filled with quicksand, hot lava, or live alligators. Add a little food coloring to tint the water red or green, or float some plastic alligators in it.

Ages: 6 and up   *Players: 4 or more*

Kiddie Carnival

Play a variety of carnival games in the pool.

Materials

Soda or soup cans

Plastic rings or rings cut from Styrofoam that float

Small balls

Bucket

Hula hoop

Balloons

Large ball or hard ball

How to Play

RING TOSS Set a number of soda or soup cans in the kiddie pool so that their tops stick up above the water's surface. Have the kids stand outside of the pool and try to throw the rings over the can tops.

TARGET BALL Set a number of plastic rings in the pool. Have the kids stand outside the pool try to toss small balls into the centers of the rings.

BUCKET BALL Fill a bucket with a little water and set it in the pool. It should be weighted, but still float. Have the kids try to shoot balls into the bucket from outside the pool.

BOUNCE BALL Set the pool by a wall. Have the kids stand a few feet from the pool and try to get the ball into the pool by bouncing it off the wall. To make it more difficult, have them bounce the ball into a floating hula hoop in the pool.

BALLOON TAG Float a bunch of balloons in the water. Have the kids stand outside the pool and try to knock a balloon out of the water by throwing a large ball. Or have them throw a hard ball to make the balloons pop.

Make sure all the kids are able to play the games and that they are not beyond any of the kids' developmental levels.

CHAPTER FOUR

SLIDES, SPRINKLERS & SOAKERS

You don't need to search the seven seas for water wonderlands. Everyone from toddlers to teenagers can have a blast on the grass right in your own backyard. All you need are a few props, a few kids, and a few suggestions, which you'll find in this chapter. We think the kids will love playing Attack of the Flying Sponges, Erupting Volcano, Snake in the Grass, and Water Weenie, but they may come up with even more ideas of their own, once they get a hold of the hose. So turn on the water, turn up the sprinkler, and go get soaked!

*A Slippery Slide is a super silly way
to keep cool on a hot day.*

Ages: 4 and up

Slippery Slide

Slip and slide on a hot day.

Materials

Plastic tablecloth, shower curtain, or sheeting (available at hardware stores)

Tent pegs

Hose and nozzle

How to Play

Lay the plastic material on the lawn. You can also use several large plastic garbage bags, cut open and taped together at the ends with plastic tape. Secure the corners with tent pegs pounded into the ground so the corners won't stick up. Place the hose nozzle on the "spray" setting and put it at one end of the plastic so that the water runs down the plastic. Then run and slip and slide.

Variation Set the slide up on an incline to make a faster slide.

Variation Play follow the leader, with one child doing a trick or stunt on the slide, then have the rest of the gang imitate her. Take turns being the leader.

Variation Have a contest to see who can stay on the slide all the way to the end without going off the sides, or make it all the way to the end without stopping.

SAFETY

Be sure tent pegs are securely in the ground and that heavy objects have no sharp points or edges that could hurt kids who slide into them. Move the slide after 30 minutes to prevent damage to your lawn.

Stay out of the way of the erupting volcano! Watch out for the hot lava! And try not to get wet!

Erupting Volcano

Try to stay dry while everyone else gets wet.

Materials

Sprinkler

Old garden hose

For Variation

Blindfolds, 1 for each player

How to Play

Set the sprinkler in the center of the lawn and turn it on. Have the players divide into two teams, with an equal number on each side. Have the teams each hold an end of the garden hose, and stand in line on either side of the sprinkler. On the word "Go!" have the two teams try to pull their opponent into the sprinkler—also known as hot lava—with the garden hose. The team that gets "sacrificed to the volcano" first loses—and gets wet.

Variation When a team wins, divide the winning team up and have them play against each other while the others watch. When the next team wins, divide that team in half and play again. Continue until you have a winner—the sole survivor of the erupting volcano.

SAFETY

Use a few sheets tied together instead of a garden hose. Sheets are softer and easier to hold.

A vigorous way to get each other wet.

Attack of the Flying Sponges

Tag someone else with a wet sponge.

Materials

Sponges in a variety of colors

Buckets of water

How to Play

Collect a bunch of inexpensive sponges from the store—the larger the better—in a variety of colors for added fun. Set out buckets of water on either side of the lawn or play area, or if possible, give a bucket of water to each player. Toss the sponges inside the buckets to get them wet. On the word "Go!" the kids grab a sponge from the bucket and chase each other around the lawn, trying to hit other players with the wet sponges.

Variation Play a version of Capture the Flag by dividing into two teams. Have buckets and sponges on both sides. Have the teams try to steal their opponent's sponges from the water buckets, without getting tagged by an opponent's flying sponge. The players can use only one sponge at a time, the rest must remain in the water bucket. If a player is tagged, he is "out." Play continues until all the other players on a team are tagged and out, too.

SAFETY

Warn the kids not to throw the sponges at anyone's face.

Variation Have only one player with a sponge bucket at one end of the play area. Have the other players try to get to the other side without being tagged by a wet sponge. Have the player defending her side throw sponges from her water bucket at the players who advance to her side. You can have one player at a time try to reach the other side, or have them all try at the same time, for a wilder game.

Variation Have the players stand in a circle, with one player in the middle, next to a bucket of sponges. Have the players on the outside try to dodge the wet sponges thrown by the player in the middle. To make it harder, have the player in the middle close his eyes. To make it even harder, have the players in the circle close their eyes, too.

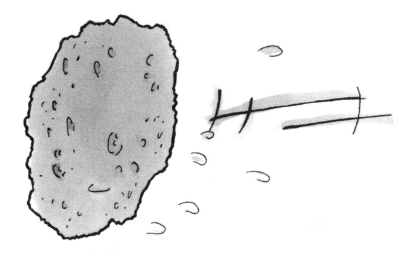

Ages: 5 and up   **Players: 2 or more**

Super Squirter

Get everyone wet!

Materials

Latex gloves

Garden hose

Rubber bands or string

For Variations

Buckets

Pin or skewer

Water balloons

Large sponges

Plastic cups and bowls

Squirt guns

Turkey basters

Plastic spray bottles

Plastic garbage can lids

How to Play

Stick a latex glove over the end of the hose and cut off the fingertips. Secure it tightly to the hose with rubber bands or string. Turn on the water and watch it spray in five different directions.

Variation Give the kids latex gloves to fill under the spigot or in a bucket of water. Poke small holes in each of the finger tips with a pin or skewer, and have the kids squeeze the gloves to make them squirt.

Variation Fill balloons with water and toss them at one another. Fill up cups and bowls and fling the water at your friends. Soak up water in sponges and toss them. Squirt everyone with squirt guns, turkey basters, or plastic spray bottles.

Variation Give all the kids a plastic garbage can lid or other shield to protect themselves from the onslaught of water, while they spray their enemies.

SAFETY

  Grown-ups should supervise wild play, so no one gets hurt. Warn the kids not to squirt each other in the face.

A high-powered homemade water squirter that goes the distance.

Water Weenie

Spray a long distance with your Water Weenie.

Materials

³/₈-inch rubber surgical tubing, 3 to 5 feet long (available at hardware stores)

Ballpoint pen

Electrical tape

Nozzle

How to Play

Buy rubber tubing at the hardware store. Tie off one end. Insert the top half of the ballpoint pen into the other end and tape it securely with electrical tape. Fill the tube slowly with water using a narrow nozzle, by inserting the end with the ballpoint pen into the water, and watch the tubing expand. Remove the nozzle when the tubing is filled and block the pen opening with your finger. Then aim and shoot and see how far you can make the stream go.

Variation Have a contest against your opponent to see who can squirt the farthest, or see whose squirter lasts the longest. Have a water war with your Water Weenies.

SAFETY

Fill the tubing slowly and carefully. Don't shoot anyone in the face.

Watch out! That's not a sprinkler—there's a snake in the grass!

Ages: 5 and up **Players: 2 or more**

Snake in the Grass

Get wet with a sprinkler in a variety of ways.

Materials

Sprinklers

Hose

How to Play

Lay the sprinkler on the lawn. Have players weave in and out of the sprinkler area, while one player turns the water on and off intermittently with his back to the players to try to get the others wet. If he catches a player and gets her wet, she is "out." When everyone is soaked, play again, with a new player turning on the sprinkler. Make a rule that a player may not spend more than five seconds away from the sprinkler, and make them count out loud.

Variation Send players through the sprinkler car wash by having them walk through the sprinkler slowly as the other players sponge them clean.

Variation Have the players dance around the yard and freeze when the sprinklers come on. Anyone who moves is out.

Variation Turn the hose into a fountain. Spray straight up in the air and try not to get wet underneath it.

SAFETY *Watch where you run and spray the water.*

62

Just add water to your Olympic feats and let the games begin.

Water Olympics

Win medals for your water feats.

Materials

Hose

Medium-size plastic ball

Something to award as a medal

How to Play

SPRINKLER JUMP Have someone hold the hose out about a foot from the ground, with a stream of water forming a "pole" to jump over. Have the other kids line up and try to jump over the water line one at a time. Repeat, raising the water line a few inches every time they jump. See who can jump over the highest water line without getting wet. Those who do get wet must drop out until there is a single winner. Award a medal.

WATER LIMBO How low can you go? Hold the hose up high, about four feet from the ground, with the water streaming straight out to form a limbo "pole." Have everyone line up and move under the water line, limbo style (facing forward, knees bent, head back) without getting wet. Repeat a second time, but lower the water line a few inches. Repeat until you have only one limbo expert left. Award a medal.

WATER WAVES Hold the hose midway and wave it slowly up and down. Have the kids line up to run through the water line as it wiggles high and low and try not to get wet. Those who are caught by the waving water are out. Continue until only one player is left. Award a medal.

WATER SNAKE Hold the hose on the pavement or lawn and move it back and forth to create a water "snake." Have the kids try to run across the lawn without getting their feet wet. Those who get "bit by the snake" are "out" until one player remains. Award a medal.

WATER JUMP ROPE Hold one end of the hose like a jump rope and circle it around to make large water circles. Have the kids run into the water rope one at a time and try to jump as high as they can without getting wet. After everyone has had a jump, turn the water rope faster for the next round. Award a medal for the highest number of jumps.

WATER BALL Have two or more players stand opposite each other with a hose and water stream in between as a "net." Have one team toss a medium-size plastic ball to the other team and continue tossing back and forth, without dropping the ball. Meanwhile, the person holding the hose can move the water net up and down to hit the ball as it goes from one side to the other. If the hoser hits the ball, she goes to the side that lost the ball and their player comes out. Or keep points and award a medal.

You don't need an ocean to go deep-sea diving.
Just a helmet and an imagination.

Diver Down

Explore your backyard deep sea.

Materials for Each Diver

Large brown paper bag

Pencil

Scissors

Blue-tinted cellophane

Clear tape

Paper towel tube, or
2 toilet paper tubes

Masking or electrical tape

2 oatmeal containers

For Variations

Magnifying glass

How to Play

Get your gear together before you go diving. Fit a large brown paper bag over a child's head. Mark where the face area is with a pencil, remove the bag, and cut out a round opening for the face with scissors. Tape a piece of blue-tinted cellophane inside the paper bag to create the mask for viewing under the sea. Cut the paper towel tube in half or use two toilet paper tubes. Set the tubes together, end to end, and tape with electrical tape, leaving ¼ inch of space, so the tube can bend slightly. Tape the tube to the paper bag. Tape two oatmeal containers together to form air tanks, and attach them to the child's back, using masking or electrical tape. Attach the other end of the air tubing to the air tanks. Now send your explorer into the deep blue sea of your backyard, so she can admire the unusual sea life, underwater plants, and shipwrecks.

Variation Have the kids lie on the ground with a magnifying glass and explore the bottom of the sea.

Variation Turn on the sprinkler to add to the excitement.

A refreshing way to use your brain on a hot day.

Game-Show Hose

Get the answer or get wet!

Materials

Hose

Trivia questions

For Variations

Die

How to Play

Get the trivia questions from a favorite guessing game, such as a kids' jeopardy or kids' trivia game. One player holds the questions and the hose, while the other players line up facing him. The player holding the hose asks one of the other players a trivia question. If the player can answer the question, she gets to take a step forward, toward the game-show host. If she is wrong, she gets squirted by the hose and has to stay where she is. Keep asking questions until someone finally makes it all the way to the player holding the hose. That contestant then becomes the game-show host, and the game-show host becomes a contestant.

Variation You don't need to have a boxed game or set of questions to play. Just make up questions for the contestants—not too hard and not too easy. You might ask questions about favorite TV shows, so that everyone has a fair chance to answer. For example, "What color is Barney?" "What are the names of Roseanne's kids?" "Name the Power Rangers." And so on.

Variation Use a die instead of questions. Roll the die and ask someone to do a task based on the roll. For example, if they get a 1 or 4, they take a step forward. If they get a 2 or 5, they take a step back. If they get a 3 or 6, they get sprayed by the hose.

SAFETY

Don't spray anyone in the face.

Set up your own shooting gallery and have a hose down.

Shooting Gallery

To shoot down the bottles with the squirt guns.

Materials

Empty plastic bottles,
Styrofoam or paper cups,
or small cereal boxes

Squirt guns

For Variations

Pinwheels

Blindfolds

How to Play

Line up plastic bottles, cups, or boxes along a table or fence. The players, holding squirt guns, should stand a distance from the line. On the word "Go!" the players shoot at the targets with their squirt guns.

Variation Let each player have a turn shooting at the target. Give them three tries to shoot a target down, then let another player have a turn.

Variation Stick toy pinwheels to the fence by taping the handles with electrical tape and see if the kids can make the pinwheels turn by squirting at them with the water guns.

Variation Have each player race to see who can shoot down a selected target first, or who can shoot down the most. Try shooting blindfolded and see how close the players can come to shooting down a target.

SAFETY

Don't use any targets that could break, such as glass.

CHAPTER FIVE

BATHTUB FUN

Do you want good, clean fun for your kids? Here's a way to make bath time entertaining—and get the kids to come clean at the same time! Just fill the tub with tips from this chapter and turn that boring bath into a fantasy fishbowl for small fry. Kids can have fun with a lot more than a rubber ducky at bath time. They can play with "spongies," cover themselves with bath body paints, make some soap shapes, or create an indoor thunderstorm.

Don't forget to scrub behind the ears!

Is it a puppet? Is it a Muppet? No!
It's a wet, washable wuppet.

Ages: 2 to 10

Water Wuppet

Make a puppet you can take in the bath.

Materials

Hand towel or 2 wash-cloths, for each puppet

Scissors

Felt-tipped permanent pen, embroidery floss and needle, or colored thread for sewing machine

2 pompoms, about 1 inch diameter (available at fabric or hobby stores)

What to Do

Using the pattern shown on page 71, with scissors cut out animal shapes from a hand towel folded in half, or from two washcloths. Draw a face with felt-tipped permanent pen, or sew on eyes, a mouth, whiskers, and so on, with a fancy machine stitch, or by hand with embroidery floss and needle. With right sides together, sew side seams, leaving the bottom edge open for the child's hand. Turn right side out. Fold up a cuff to hold soap or small toys and topstitch around outside edge. Add a pompom for the nose and one for the tail. Now you're ready to run a bath and start the Wuppet Show.

Variation Kids can make several different animal wuppets and put on a wuppet show in the bathtub. Encourage them to use their imaginations to create friendly monsters, silly animals, or likenesses of their own family members.

SAFETY

Be sure anything sewn on is attached securely so it won't come loose in the tub.

Ages: 3 to 10

Spongies

Make a collection of sponge toys for bathtub play.

Materials

Sponges

Black felt-tipped permanent pen

Scissors

What to Do

You can buy precut sponges if you prefer; these are usually found at hobby or toy stores. But they're easy to make and you can personalize your own collection if you do it yourself. Gather a variety of sponges in different sizes and colors. Using a black felt-tipped permanent pen, draw different kinds of sea-life shapes, such as flounders, sharks, jellyfishes, octopuses, alligators, eels, whales, sardines, sea horses, and clams. Add detail to the sea life: eyes, mouths, gills, spots, and so on. Then cut out the shapes using scissors. Place the spongies in the bath and let your child press them to the sides of the tub or the tile walls. Spongies will stick when the water is pressed out.

Variation Cut out likenesses of family members and pets, assorted animals, dinosaurs, or other living things, and let the kids create their own sponge world.

Variation Cut out basic geometric shapes, such as circles, squares, triangles, and rectangles, as well as other shapes, like stars, moons, and flowers. Let the kids create buildings, towns, cars, spaceships, or their own ideas, with the different shapes on the tub or tile.

Variation Help your child learn by cutting out numbers or alphabet letters. He can write his name, add or subtract, or sing the alphabet song as he plays in the tub.

SAFETY

Make sure the pieces are large enough so they can't be lost down the drain or swallowed by young children.

You can create an indoor rainstorm with this simple-to-make toy.

Thunderstorm

Get yourself wet with your own thunderstorm.

Materials

Plastic bottle (like a shampoo or dish-washing liquid bottle)

Metal skewer

For Variations

Felt-tipped permanent pens and puffy paints

Tiny toys

SAFETY

Do not use bottles that contained a harsh chemical, bathroom disinfectant, ammonia, or any other toxic substances.

What to Do

Thoroughly clean a plastic bottle, or purchase one from the drug store. Pierce a cluster of holes with a skewer on one side. Fill with water and put on the cap. Kids can raise the bottle over their heads, holey side up, turn it over, and squeeze—thunderstorm!

Variation Tint the water with blue food coloring to make it stormy looking. Decorate the outside of the plastic bottle with cloud shapes drawn with felt-tipped permanent pens and puffy paints. Float little toys inside the bottle, too.

Variation Take the storm maker out to the yard and water the plants, or use it for an outdoor water fight with your friends.

73

Ahoy there, matey! It's time to scrub the deck—er, neck.
But first, let's build a pirate ship.

Ages: 4 and up

Pirate Ship

Sail away into the tub, ye swab.

Materials

Half-gallon milk carton

12-inch strip of wood-grained adhesive plastic (like Contac)

Scissors

2 plastic margarine tub lids

Waterproof glue

3 plastic straws

Three 3-inch squares of colorful fabric or paper

Clear adhesive plastic

Colored plastic tape

Cutouts or decals

Metal skewer or other sharp instrument

2 short lengths of yarn

What to Do

Rinse and dry the milk carton and cover it with wood-grained adhesive plastic. Use scissors to make a cut, 1 inch from the bottom, through one side of carton, extending 1 inch down the sides (see illustration page 75). Make a slit at the top. Fold in the sides and top to make a deck. Cut three small circles from each plastic lid and glue to the sides of the ship with waterproof glue. Make three 1-inch-long

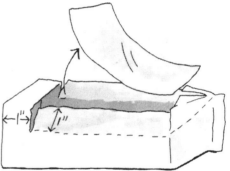

cuts in one end of each of the plastic straws and fold ends out. Glue

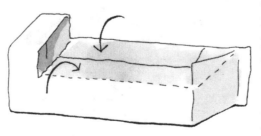

ends to the deck. Cut three 3-inch squares of colorful fabric or paper and cover both sides with clear adhesive plastic. Make a slit near the top and bottom of each square and slip them over the straws; the squares should bow slightly like sails. Add decorations, using decals or cutouts made from plastic tape. Poke holes with a metal skewer in the tops of the two outside straws and in the ends of the carton to attach yarn.

Variation Create the boat you want, using the basic milk carton materials and your imagination. Make a sailing ship, a Viking ship, the *Mayflower*, a catamaran, or your own creation. Use a picture from the library book on boats for inspiration and ideas.

SAFETY

Make sure there are no sharp edges on the boats, and that young children don't swallow the small pieces.

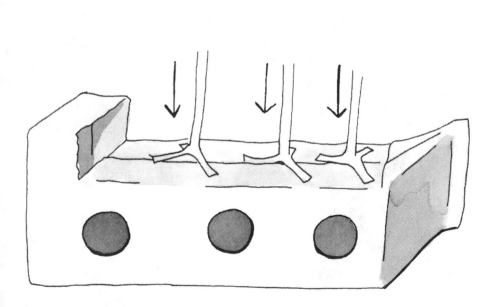

Here's a way to recycle those inflatable summer toys that seem barely to last the season.

Ages: 4 and up

Sticker Magic

Decorate your bathroom tub and tile with stick-on plastic cutouts.

Materials

Old popped beach ball, air mattress, plastic inner tube, or plastic sheeting (available at hardware stores)

Scissors

For Variations

Cookie sheet

Heavy-duty plastic wrap

Clear tape

Picture books or comic books

Clear adhesive plastic (like Contac)

What to Do

Cut old plastic materials with scissors into a variety of shapes or designs. You might want to cut out geometric shapes, alphabet letters, numbers, cartoon characters, household items, landscape items, or anything your child enjoys. Place the cutouts on the side of a wet tub or tile wall so your child can spell words, make up a town, or have some make-believe adventures.

Variation You can also cover the inside of a cookie sheet with heavy-duty plastic wrap, tape it down to secure it, and use the cookie sheet as a background to create a fantasy world.

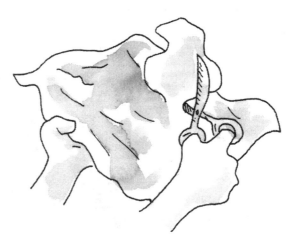

Variation Cut out pictures from your child's favorite picture book (make sure it's an extra!), comic book, or other source of illustrations. Cut off a foot-long piece of clear adhesive plastic, peel off the protective paper, and set it, sticky side up, on the table. Place the cartoon cutouts on the sticky side, at least an inch apart. Carefully cover with a second sheet of clear adhesive plastic, sticky side down. Cut out cartoon characters leaving ¼ to ½ inch all around the outside of the cutout so that the sticky plastic sticks to itself in the water and doesn't come undone. Place the cutouts on the side of a wet tub or tile wall and watch them stick. Your child can use her imagination to play with the cartoon characters.

SAFETY

Make sure the pieces are large enough so they can't be lost down the drain or swallowed by young children.

Here's a chance to make cleaning up an art.

Ages: 4 to 10

Body Paints

Paint your body like a canvas.

Materials

Body paints

Plastic mixing bowl

Shaving cream

Food coloring

Popsicle stick

Hand lotion

Shampoo

Nonbreakable mirror

Large soft-bristle paint-brushes

Watercolor paints

SAFETY

Tell the kids not to paint on or near their faces.

What to Do

There are many commercial multicolored body paints on the market. They can be purchased at stores that sell bath products, as well as toy stores, drug stores, and hobby stores. But you can make your own paints using one of the following methods.

SHAVING CREAM Shake up a can of shaving cream and squirt some into a bowl. Tint the shaving cream with food coloring, stir it up well, and let the kids spread it over their bodies. Offer a Popsicle stick for them to "shave" themselves.

HAND LOTION Squirt a handful of hand lotion in a bowl and tint it with food coloring. Let the kids fingerpaint it all over their bodies. Rinse off with soap and water in the shower when bath time is over.

SHAMPOO Mix a capful of shampoo with water and a few drops of food coloring in a plastic bowl. Mix up several bowls of different colors, if desired. Place a nonbreakable mirror near the tub and let your child paint his body with the shampoo using large soft-bristle paint-brushes. Rinse off the paint between colors, or leave the different colors on for a patchwork look.

WATERCOLORS Use a small watercolor paint palette in the bath and let the kids paint themselves with the watercolors. Rinse off when bath time is over.

Ages: 4 and up

Icebergs

Watch the iceberg melt.

Materials

Empty half-gallon milk carton or other container (see below)

Food coloring

Little plastic toys

What to Do

Fill a clean half-gallon milk carton full of water tinted with food coloring. You can also use ice-cube trays or Popsicle, gelatin, or other molds for making ice shapes. Freeze overnight, until solid. Fill the tub with warm water, tear off the milk carton container or remove ice from molds, and place in the tub. Give your child small plastic toys to set on the iceberg and watch them fall off as the ice melts.

Variation Make ice cubes all different colors. Put them in the tub at the same time and see which colors melt first. Place bets on favorite colors. See how long it takes the cubes to melt by timing them.

Variation Make a rainbow iceberg. Fill a half-gallon milk carton a quarter full with water tinted with blue food coloring. Freeze until solid. Fill another quarter with red-tinted water and freeze. Repeat with yellow- and green-tinted water. When all the layers are frozen, peel off the milk carton and place the rainbow boat in the bath water. The milk carton gives it a boat shape.

Variation Place little toys, such as plastic animals, people, or monsters, inside the tinted water-filled molds before freezing. Freeze overnight, until firm, then place in the tub. Watch the toys appear as the ice melts.

SAFETY

Keep an eye on younger children when they play with little toys. Make sure the bath water is warm so that the kids don't get cold when the ice melts and the water cools off.

Water is an open-ended toy in itself. Just fill the tub with lots of gadgets and watch the kids enjoy themselves for hours.

Tub Buddies

Explore the properties of water.

Materials

Stones

Leaves and flowers

Fabric swatches

Wooden blocks

Kitchen items (see below)

Finger paints

Sponges

Plastic bowls and containers

Corks

Straws or plastic tubing

Baster

Waterproof baby doll

What to Do

There are so many things to do in the bathwater. Here are some suggestions:

SINK AND FLOAT Have your child walk around the house with you, picking out a variety of small items that can safely go into the bathtub. Hopefully you'll have some that sink, like plastic toys, and some that float, like corks. Set the items up along the rim of the tub before you place them in the water. Have your child guess which ones will sink and which ones will float. As he says "Sink!" or "Float!" have him drop the item into the bathwater and find out for himself.

CHANGING COLORS Get a variety of items from the yard or the house that may change colors when wet. Small, smooth stones are especially good, and so are leaves, fabric swatches, and wooden blocks. Ask your child if he thinks the item will change color or not, then have him drop that item into the water and find out. There are some toys and fabrics on the market today that change color when wet, which might be fun to try.

TEA PARTY Let your child use a bunch of kitchen items in the bath and have his own cooking school or tea party. Water offers a lot of fun when used with kitchen tools, so let him use his imagination and whip up whatever he wants. You might include an egg beater, turkey baster, some plastic sandwich bags, spatula, ladle, ice-cube tray, plastic

SAFETY

Make sure nothing breakable or sharp is in the tub. Tell him to make-believe when he eats or drinks at his tea party. Always supervise a child in the bath and don't leave him unattended.

measuring cups and spoons, and whatever else is in the kitchen that's safe in the water with kids.

WRITING ON THE WALL Let your child write on the tub or tile wall using finger paints. After the bath is over, rinse off the tub and tile with water.

OTHER FUN Give your child a sponge, and let him wash his baby doll and give it a nice bath. Give him paintbrushes and let him paint himself, the tub, and the tile walls. Give him sponges and let him clean himself, the tub, and the tile walls. Give him some straws or plastic tubing and let him blow bubbles in the tub, or let him dip underwater, using the plastic tubing as a breathing apparatus.

You can make your own soap to use in the tub.

Soap Shapes

Create your own soap shapes.

Materials

1 cup soap flakes (like Ivory Snow)

½ cup boiling water

Food coloring

Scented oil

Hand mixer or egg beater

Cookie cutters

Waxed paper

For Variation

Peppermint flavoring

Glitter

What to Do

Pour soap flakes into a large bowl. Add boiling water and stir until mixture is a thick liquid. Add food coloring and scented oil. Beat with a hand mixer or egg beater until the mixture is whipped up smooth and silky. Use metal cookie cutters with deep sides. Place cookie cutters on waxed paper and fill with soap mixture. Allow to dry. Remove soap from cookie cutters and drop into the bath.

Variation Add peppermint flavoring, not to eat, but to give the soap a nice fresh smell. Add a sprinkling of glitter to the top of the mixture in the cookie cutters to give the soap a sparkle. Add two or three colors to one cookie cutter for a rainbow soap.

SAFETY

The soap may look good enough to eat but it isn't. Tell kids to keep it in the tub and out of their mouths.

You can open your own hair salon right in your own bathtub!
Time for a cut, wash, and set.

Hair Salon

Shape your pompadour at the bathtub salon.

Materials

No-tears shampoo for children

Wide-tooth comb, brush, Popsicle sticks, chopsticks, and pencils

Food coloring

Nonbreakable mirror

What to Do

Pour a small amount of shampoo into your hands and apply to the child's head. Tint with a little food coloring. Place a nonbreakable mirror nearby so your child can see her creations. Once you've worked up a good lather, let your child create different hair styles with her hands, or let her use the comb, brush, Popsicle sticks, chopsticks, and pencils. Before she's done, take some snapshots of her creations for the family photo album.

Variation Use the shampoo to make a mustache, beard, sideburns, hairy chest, or other body decorations.

SAFETY

Be careful your child doesn't get shampoo into her eyes.

CHAPTER SIX

WATER TABLE

What's a water table? It's anything that's large enough and shallow enough to hold water. You might use an old sandbox, a plastic swimming pool, washtubs, or buy a real water table from a toy or school supply store. You can even make your own with a few pieces of plywood and some water seal. Then fill it up with you-know-what and try out the "Billions of Bubbles," "Undersea City," "Water Wax Museum," or "Watercolors" activities.

Bubbles are fascinating to kids. Luckily there are billions of ways to have fun with bubbles.

Ages: 4 and up

Billions of Bubbles

Make bubbles in many creative ways.

Materials

1 to 2 cups dish-washing liquid (Dawn works best)

2 to 4 ounces glycerin (available at the drug store)

Metal hanger

Plastic holder from a six-pack

Stick

Stapler

Pipe cleaners

Straws

Tape

Styrofoam cups

Rings from canning jar lids

Plastic berry baskets

Funnels

3 empty cans or round plastic containers

String, 3 feet

What to Do

Fill the water table with approximately 10 to 12 cups of cold water. If you don't have a water table, use a kiddie pool. Double the recipe if you double the amount of water. Add dish-washing liquid and glycerin and mix into the water. Glycerin makes the bubbles stronger and longer lasting.

METAL HANGER Twist a metal hanger or other stiff wire into different shapes—round, square, oval, rectangle, even curved. Dip the hanger into the bubble solution and gently pull it out. Let the air catch the solution as you wave it in the wind to make giant bubbles in the shape of your reconstructed hanger.

SIX-PACK HOLDER Attach a stick to a plastic six-pack holder using staples. Holding the stick, dip the plastic holder into the solution, then wave in the wind to create a half-dozen bubbles all at once.

PIPE CLEANERS Create different shapes of blowers using pipe cleaners. Connect several pipe cleaners together and make one giant blower, or twist a lot of small holes and link them together. Wave this bubble maker in the wind.

STRAWS Collect a small amount of solution in a cup and let the kids use straws to blow bubbles into the solution. Or let the kids use the straws as bubble blowers at the water table. Tape several straws together to get multiple bubbles. (To prevent the kids from sucking in the liquid, cut a small slit at the top of the straw. This allows the kids to blow but not inhale.)

STYROFOAM CUPS Cut a hole in the bottom of a Styrofoam cup and dip into solution. Use it to blow a large bubble.

RINGS FROM JAR LIDS Try using rings from canning jar lids to make bubbles, or anything else from the kitchen that might work, such as a turkey baster, bacon tongs, potato masher, and egg beater.

BERRY BASKETS Berry baskets make billions of tiny bubbles. Just dip the basket into the solution and wave it in the wind.

FUNNELS Try dipping both ends of a funnel into the solution—one at a time. Blow at the end opposite the solution and see what different sizes of bubbles you can get.

CANS Tape three cans or plastic containers together with electrical tape to form a long tube. Use to blow giant bubbles.

STRING Cut a 3-foot-long piece of string. Thread two straws onto the string, and tie the string together. Separate the two straws and move them to opposite sides of the string, with an equal amount between them. Dip the string into the bubble solution and pull out a great big bubble. You can also use a hula hoop for a similar effect.

For Variations

Cotton mittens or gloves
Soup can, unopened
Food coloring
Small mixing bowl
Poster paints
White construction paper

Make sure the kids don't inhale the bubble solution or get it in their eyes. Check to see that the edges of all the blowers are smooth. Cover with electrical tape, if necessary.

Variation Have a Bubble Juggle. Put on a pair of cotton mittens or gloves, or dip your hands into the bubble solution. Dip a blower into the bubble solution and blow a bubble. Cup your hand and gently move the bubble into your palm. Bounce the bubble into the air and see how many times you can juggle it before it pops.

Variation Have the kids race their bubbles to a finish line. If his bubble pops, the player must stop for a moment and blow another one. All players continue racing until someone reaches the finish line with an unpopped bubble.

Variation Blow a bubble onto the surface of the water tray. Leave the straw inside the bubble, and blow another bubble. Admire your double bubble.

Variation Two kids can make a giant bubble by blowing together. Have the kids blow two separate bubbles in the water table using hollow cans, then connect the two bubbles into one single bubble. Keep blowing the big bubble until it pops.

Variation Tint the water with food coloring to turn it pink, green, or blue for fun.

Variation Pour a small amount of bubble solution into a small bowl and add some poster paint. Blow tiny bubbles using a straw, then capture them on paper by pressing a sheet of white construction paper over them. Lift the paper and see the bubble design you have printed. Repeat with a new color.

Variation Substitute ½ cup Karo syrup for glycerin, if desired. This solution may leave a sticky residue, however.

*Let the kids build their own underwater
world with ever popular Legos.*

Ages: 5 and up

Undersea City

Create a unique landscape using Legos underwater.

Materials

Legos or other plastic
building pieces

Double-sided tape

Feathers, pipe cleaners,
pieces of plastic wrap in
various colors, crinkle
paper, metallic confetti,
small balls, and little plastic people or animals

For Variations

Clay

SAFETY

*Make sure you use
only building materials that
water will not dissolve or
ruin.*

What to Do

Empty the water table (or kiddie pool) and dry completely. Place
double-sided tape on the bottom of the water table and press down a
number of Lego boards (the flat plastic boards that create the foundation of Lego buildings). Fill the water table with water and let the kids
build with Legos. Give them feathers, pipe cleaners, plastic wrap, crinkle paper, and other small objects to add to their structures.

Variation Try using clay underwater, or drawing a roadway on a
plastic shower curtain placed underwater and letting the kids drive little cars underwater. Let them have a road race and watch the water
impede their speed.

Create your own works of wax art by adding a little water.

Water Wax Museum

Watch the surprising sculpture that appears when wax hits water.

Materials

Disposable aluminum pie tin

Pot holders

Colored wax: old or new candles, or wax-making materials

For Variations

Crayons

Aluminum foil

Muffin tin

SAFETY

Grown-up supervision is very important! Hot wax is very dangerous, so use caution when handling hot tins of wax. Use pot holders that can get wet to carry the pans and submerge them into the water.

What to Do

Fill the water table or a tub with cold water. In an aluminum pie tin melt colored wax over a double boiler. You can use old candles, buy new candles, or buy wax-making materials from a hobby store. When the wax is completely melted, use pot holders and quickly but carefully dunk the pan into the cold water. Hold the pan in the water for about 30 seconds. When you take the pan out of the water, you will have an interesting wax sculpture.

Variation Use peeled color crayons in similar shades with a small cube of paraffin wax for every six to eight crayons, instead of colored wax.

Variation Using aluminum foil, create sections in the pan. Fill each compartment with a variety of colors. Melt the wax and dunk it into the cold water.

Variation Use a muffin tin and fill each cup with a different color. Plunge into the cold water.

Variation Slowly drizzle hot wax from the pie tin into the cold water. Watch the free-form design appear.

Hey! This isn't water! Well, if it isn't, what is it?

It's Not Water!

See what happens to water when you add a few other ingredients.

Materials

2 mixing bowls

Fruit-flavored gelatin

Large pan

Vanilla instant pudding

Food coloring

Cornstarch

White glue

Borax

For Variation

Plastic sealable bags

What to Do

If you have a small water table, this will work well. If it's large, place a large pan in the middle of the empty water table. Give the kids utensils to help them explore the It's-Not-Water concoctions.

GELATIN Mix up several packages of fruit-flavored gelatin in a mixing bowl, according to package directions. Fill a large pan with the gelatin and set it in the refrigerator to firm. When the gelatin is somewhat set, pour the gelatin into the water table. Let the kids play with the semi-soft gelatin.

PUDDING Make up several packages of vanilla instant pudding according to the package directions. Pour into a large pan and set in the water table. Let the kids explore the properties of pudding with their hands. Add food coloring if desired.

MAGIC MOOSH Combine 2 cups cornstarch with ½ cup water. Add food coloring and mix well with your hands. The magic concoction changes from dry to wet, from hard to soft, from firm to slimy, and from white to colored. Kids will have fun squeezing this mixture in their hands and feeling it grow firm, then relaxing their hands and feeling it turn to slime.

SQUEEZABLE STUFF Make sure the kids are there to watch you make this strange stuff. In one bowl combine 2 cups white glue and 1½ cups water. Mix well. In a second bowl combine 1~ cups water and 4 teaspoons borax. Now combine the contents of both bowls in a large

Squeezable Stuff will not wash out of fabric, so limit its use to the water table. Make sure the kids know the difference between the stuff they can taste (gelatin and pudding), and the stuff they can't (cornstarch and glue).

pan in the water table at the same time and watch what happens. Then let the kids play with it.

Variation Mix all the It's-Not-Water products in the water table, then pour amounts into small plastic sealable bags for individual use. Seal the bags and let the kids feel the mixture through the plastic.

*This make-it-yourself toy has two uses—
in the sand and in the water.*

Ages: 4 and up

Sand and Water Wheel

Make a wheel to move sand and water.

Materials

Half-gallon milk carton

Scissors

8-ounce plastic yogurt container

Tagboard or cardboard

Clear adhesive plastic (like Contac)

White glue

Chopstick or similar wooden stick

Small funnel

Small cup

✚
SAFETY
Cutting the milk carton with scissors requires grown-up assistance or supervision.

What to Do

Clean out a half-gallon milk carton and cut two holes opposite each other, one on each side of the carton in the middle. Fold in the top of the carton. Cut out a circle in the top to hold the funnel. Cut a 1-inch-wide ring from a plastic yogurt container. From tagboard, cut out eight 2-by-1-inch strips. Cover the strips with clear adhesive plastic and fold the strips in half. Glue the strips around the outside of the plastic ring. Allow the wheel to dry.

Poke a hole in either side of the milk carton. Place the wheel inside carton, and insert a chopstick or other wooden stick through the carton holes and the center of the wheel. Rest a small funnel in the hole at the top of the carton, being sure it does not hit the wheel. (If your funnel is too long, lower the wheel.) Place a small cup inside at the bottom of the container. Drop sand or pour water through the funnel at the top and watch it turn the wheel and empty into the cup at the bottom.

Variation Add other obstacles to your water wheel along the way. You might want to include slides, tunnels, twists, barriers, ramps, holes, and so on.

It's time to give the baby a bath!

Baby Bath

Take care of your baby doll.

Materials

Baby doll

Dirt

Eye droppers

Cups and bowls

Sponges and washcloths

Small soaps and baby shampoo

Plastic baby bottles

Baby-doll-size cups and bottles

What to Do

Find a baby doll that can get wet. The best ones are those that drink, wet, and have washable hair. Fill the water table with warm water. Put a little dirt on the baby here and there. Tell your child the baby is dirty and needs a bath. Then let your child use the accessories listed above to clean the baby in the water table. Your child can also feed the baby with a small baby bottle or drinking cup.

Variation If you've got an agreeable pet, you might give it a bath.

SAFETY

Grown-up supervision is important to protect the safety of both your child and the pet!

*Turn your water table into an indoor sandbox on rainy days
when the kids can't go out and play—or any time!*

Ages: 4 and up

Rainy Day Sandbox

Make an indoor sandbox.

Materials

Sand

Cornmeal, farina (Cream of Wheat), oatmeal, cereals, seeds, grains, beans, dried coffee grounds, popcorn, or Styrofoam pellets

Toys for sand and water

What to Do

Empty and dry the water table. Fill it with sand or any of the other items listed under Materials for variety. Collect a bunch of toys for sand and water and let the kids do whatever they want.

Variation Add a little water to the sandbox and see what happens.

Variation Combine a variety of the materials listed above to create a varied texture.

Variation Show the kids how to rake the sand, draw shapes, outline handprints, make impressions, write their names, sift, pour, dig, and bury.

✚ SAFETY

Don't allow the kids to eat any of the materials. Use only nontoxic materials. Remind the kids not to throw the materials so they won't get in anyone's eyes.

95

Create works of art with colored water.

Watercolors

Experiment with color in the water table.

Materials

Food coloring, finger paints, poster paints, or watercolors

Spoon or eyedropper

Brushes

For Variation

White construction paper

What to Do

Clean out the water table and dry it completely. Pour a small amount of food coloring, finger paints, or watercolors into the bottom of the tray. Make several pools of different colors with space between them. Let the kids add a little water with a spoon or eyedropper, and paint the bottom of the water table with the brushes and the pools of color.

Variation Let the kids use their hands instead of brushes to smear the colors on the bottom of the tray.

Variation Add a thin layer of water to the water table first, then add the food coloring or other paints.

Variation After the artwork is completed, press a large sheet of white construction paper on top of the painting to reproduce it. Hang the picture up to dry while you clean the water table.

SAFETY

Make sure you use nontoxic colors that will wash out, if the kids are using their hands instead of the brushes. Remind them to keep the colors inside the water table and not to paint anything else!

*You can create your own underwater
garden right in your water table.*

Underwater Bouquet

Make a water garden of flowers.

Materials

Plastic or real flowers

Modeling clay

What to Do

Collect some plastic or real flowers and cut them so they have stems about 2 inches long. Remove any leaves from the lower part of the stems. Place small balls of clay in the water table. Let the kids plant the flowers into the clay, creating special arrangements, walkways, flower mazes, or designs. When the flower garden is finished, fill the tray with water and admire your underwater wonderland.

Variation Float lily pads, real or cut from plastic, on top of the pond. Add boats to float on the pond, too.

Variation Re-create these flower gardens in small plastic or glass jars, such as baby food jars, as a tiny keepsake underwater flower garden for your child. Attach the clay to the inside of the lid, add tiny flowers, then fill the jar with water, close and seal lid, and turn over to enjoy the water garden.

SAFETY

Try to use plastic jars if you have them, so they won't break if dropped.

CHAPTER SEVEN

WATER ACTIVITIES

Water is an amazing substance—kids can do so many things with it! The possibilities for wet and wild fun are plentiful. Here are a few suggestions for water activities the kids can do in- or outdoors, in hot or cold weather. All they require are a few props and some imagination. Start with the "Dancing Water Bugs," "Frozen Slushies," "Ice Balloons," or "Musical Mud Puddles" to get the kids active in the water.

*Share your water with a feathered
friend—make a birdbath!*

Birdbath

Create a birdbath in your own yard.

Materials

Half-gallon milk carton

Scissors

Sand, stones, or a brick

Shallow plastic bowl

What to Do

Rinse out the milk carton and cut off the top with scissors. Find a site in your yard that is not too busy so the birds will feel safe when they come to visit. Set the milk carton there as a base for the birdbath. Fill the base with sand, stones, or a brick to make it steady. Set a plastic bowl on top and add a few stones to the bottom of the bowl to anchor it to the base. Fill with water and watch as the birds come and take a dip when they discover the new neighborhood pool.

Variation Make a birdfeeder the same way, except fill it with birdseed instead of water. Set it near the birdbath so you'll attract even more birds.

Variation Build a birdhouse out of a milk carton and some twine and attach it to the fence or a tree. When the birds come to take a bath, they'll find room and board at your luxury bird bed-and-breakfast.

SAFETY

Grown-ups should assist with cutting the milk carton.

Create a work of art using frozen water.

Ice Sculpture

Chip a sculpture out of ice.

Materials

Large bowl, carton, or tray

Plastic screening or plastic garbage bag

Glitter or candy sprinkles

For Variations

Plastic action figure or animal

Fruit juice or fruit-flavored drink

Containers with interesting shapes (see below)

Food coloring

Chisel or dull butter knife

Small hammer

What to Do

Fill a large container with water and place it in the freezer. Freeze overnight, until firm. When frozen, release ice from the container onto plastic sheeting or a plastic garbage bag laid on the lawn. (To release ice, run the container under warm water for a few seconds.) Give the kids a chisel or butter knife and a small hammer and let them chip away at the ice to make an interesting sculpture. Tell them to work quickly before their material melts away!

Variation Have them create their ice sculptures using only their hands and mouths.

SAFETY

Teach the kids how to hold the chisel and hammer so they won't hurt themselves. Have them use spoons instead of chisels or knives, if you prefer.

Variation Add food coloring to the water before it freezes so your ice sculpture has a pink, blue, or green tint to it. Add glitter or candy sprinkles, too, for an interesting look.

Variation Play Rescue the Abominable Snowman. Fill container half full and freeze overnight, until firm. Place a tiny plastic action figure or animal on top of the frozen surface, add more water to fill the container, and freeze again. Have the kids race to get the frozen person or animal freed from the "iceberg."

Variation Have the kids make small sculptures out of ice cubes or blocks of ice. Freeze fruit juice or fruit-flavored drink and let the kids carve the sculpture using their teeth.

Variation Gather a bunch of containers that have interesting shapes, such as a rubber glove, a scooped-out orange, cake or gelatin mold, plastic food containers, ice-cube trays, or balloons. Fill with water and freeze overnight. Release the ice from the containers and let the kids put together an ice sculpture using the different ice shapes.

Make your own musical instruments using water.

Water Music

Create your own music with water-filled containers.

Materials

Glass drinking glasses

Spoons

For Variations

Empty glass soda bottles

Small water bottles with lids

Beads

Metal or hollow objects for noise-making (see below)

Wineglasses

SAFETY Make sure the kids handle the glass containers carefully.

What to Do

Find five or six identical drinking glasses and fill them to different levels with water. Line them up on the table, from lowest water level to highest water level. Give each kid a spoon to tap out a tune on the sides of the glasses. Tell them to listen to the different notes each glass creates. Ask the kids this question: Do you need more or less water in the glass to make a higher note?

Variation Fill five or six empty glass soda bottles with different levels of water. Line them up from lowest water level to highest water level. Have the kids blow gently across the tops of the bottles to make different musical notes. Have them try to blow a simple song or create a marching band.

Variation To complete your band, fill small water bottles half full with water. Replace lids and shake bottles to make a percussion sound. Add beads to create a new sound.

Variation Make spray drums by using plastic metal lids, aluminum pie tins, and cans, as well as jugs, flowerpots, or other hollow noise-makers. Set them up against a fence and spray with a hose or plastic spraybottle to make sounds.

Variation Make your wineglasses whistle by filling a number of glasses with water. Have each kid wet a finger and run it around the rim of the glass, pressing lightly. Go around several times and soon you will hear a haunting whistle from the glass.

*Everyone knows what a water balloon is.
Have you ever seen an ice balloon?*

Ages: 4 and up

Ice Balloons

Explore the properties of ice balloons.

Materials

Water balloons

Large tub, cooler, kiddie pool, or water table

For Variations

Rubber bands or string

Food coloring

Small plastic toys

Tape

Needle

What to Do

Fill water balloons three-quarters full with water (don't overfill!) and place them in the freezer overnight, until firm. Fill an extra balloon with water and do not freeze it. Fill a large tub, cooler, kiddie pool, or water table with water. Give each child a frozen balloon and let the kids examine them. Then ask if they think the ice balloons will sink or float. Let the kids place the balloons in the water and watch what happens. Compare the frozen balloons to the water balloon and see which sink or float.

Variation Have the kids hold the ice balloons for a few minutes and let their warm hands melt the balloons into unusual shapes. Have them pop the balloons and peel them. Let them place the ice into the water tub again and watch them float or sink, and melt.

Variation Tie the balloons off with a bunch of rubber bands or string to create new shapes, then freeze. See what kinds of weird shapes you get when you unpeel the balloons.

Variation Tint the water with food coloring before freezing the balloon and watch the kids' surprise as they peel off the balloons.

Variation Place a few small toys in the balloon before you fill it. Fill it three-quarters with water and freeze. The kids will enjoy seeing the hidden toys inside the ice balloons and retrieving them when the ice has melted.

Variation Try a magic trick. Fill a balloon with water. Place a small piece of tape on the balloon. Poke a needle through the tape and balloon. It doesn't pop! Remove needle and squirt the water out through the tiny hole.

*Let the kids create their own ice caves, complete
with stalactites and stalagmites.*

Ages: 4 and up

Ice Caves

See how ice melts and creates various designs.

Materials
Bowl

Plate

Small paper cups

Food coloring

Eye droppers

Salt

For Variation
Black paper

White paper

What to Do

Pour water into a bowl and freeze overnight, until firm. Remove the bowl from the freezer and release ice by running the bowl under warm water for a few seconds. Place ice on a plate and take it outside. Fill small paper cups with water and a few drops of food coloring. Give the kids eye droppers and let them fill the droppers with the colored water. Have them squeeze the droppers onto the dome of ice and see what happens as the water melts the ice and the color remains. Sprinkle salt onto the ice and use the eye droppers again. Watch the different shapes appear as the salt and food coloring melt the ice.

Variation See how long it takes two domes of ice to melt. Place two domes in the sunlight. Cover one with black paper and one with white paper. The dome under black paper should melt faster since black absorbs heat. The one under white paper should melt more slowly since white reflects heat. Time the melting and see.

SAFETY

Use caution when removing a big block of ice from the bowl. It'll be easy to lose control of it since it's slippery.

*Turn water into a great treat to eat—
or drink—during hot summer days.*

Frozen Slushies

Make your own slushies.

Materials

Paper cup or plastic container

Fruit juice or fruit-flavored drink

Spoons

For Variations

Fresh fruit

Blender

Ice-cube trays

Oranges

Latex glove

Large bowl

What to Do

Clean containers and make sure they have no sharp edges. Fill each with fruit juice or fruit-flavored drink and place in the freezer for two hours. Remove from freezer and stir with spoon. Return to freezer for another half hour. Remove, stir again, and serve right from the container with a spoon.

Variation Freeze fruit, such as grapes, raspberries, strawberries, or bananas, until firm. Whirl in the blender with a little juice and some ice cubes until slushy, and pour into cups. Serve each cup with a spoon.

Variation Make Popsicles using fruit juice or fruit-flavored drink poured into ice-cube trays with Popsicle sticks added. Drop a small piece of fruit into each compartment of the tray before filling, for a fruity surprise.

Variation Scoop out the inside of an orange. Slice a little of the peel off the bottom to create a flat surface. Fill the orange with orange juice or other fruit juice. Freeze for two hours. Stir. Freeze another half an hour. Serve in the peel with a spoon.

Variation Fill a new, clean latex glove with red fruit juice or fruit-flavored drink. Tie off the end securely and freeze overnight, until firm. Fill a large bowl with the juice and serve to the kids with the frozen "hand" in the punch bowl for an entertaining effect.

Ages: 3 and up

Dancing Water Bugs

Watch the chemical reaction in water that causes the raisins to dance.

Materials

Pint-size plastic or glass jar

Vinegar

Raisins

Baking soda

For Variation

Food coloring

What to Do

Fill the container with water. Add 3 or 4 tablespoons of vinegar and stir. Add five or six raisins and watch them sink to the bottom. Add 1 tablespoon of baking soda without stirring, and watch the "water bugs" do their dance. Why do they dance? Because bubbles of carbon dioxide form when soda, a base, is mixed with vinegar, an acid. The bubbles cling to the raisins, making them rise and fall for up to an hour.

Variation Add food coloring to the water.

✚ *SAFETY*

Use caution when mixing the solution since it reacts quickly and can over-flow if you use too much.

Paint the house, fence, or sidewalk
with your special paints.

Water Paints

Do some painting outdoors.

Materials

Pail or bucket

Food coloring

Large paintbrushes

For Variations

Small brushes, paint rollers, brooms, and sponges

What to Do

Fill up a pail or bucket with water and add a few drops of food coloring. Take the kids outside with the pail or bucket and paintbrushes. Let them paint the side of the house, the fence, or the sidewalk with the colored water. Have the kids paint their names, draw designs, or create mazes for other kids to follow. The color isn't permanent and will only last a few minutes.

Variation Use a variety of paint applicators—such as small brushes, paint rollers, brooms, and sponges.

Variation Have the kids write sentences and see who finishes a sentence first before the beginning of their sentence disappears.

Variation Have the kids paint pictures and let the other kids guess what they are drawing. Take turns so everyone has a chance to draw a picture and guess what the others' pictures represent.

Here's a variation of the ever-popular game, Musical Chairs.
This time it's Musical Mud Puddles.

Musical Mud Puddles

Land in a "mud puddle" first.

Materials

Large plastic pans, buckets, or dishpans

Harmonica or other musical instrument

What to Do

Find a plastic container for each player that's large enough for the kids to sit inside. Fill the containers with water. Set them in a circle and have the kids form another circle around the outside. Have the kids walk around the containers while you play the harmonica. When you stop playing, have the kids quickly find a "mud puddle" and fall in. Now, remove one pan and play again. This time when you stop the music the kids must scramble for the remaining mud puddles. Since there's one less, a player will be "out" when the rest of the players find their mud puddles. Remove another pan with each turn until you only have one player left.

+ SAFETY

Make sure the containers you use for mud puddles have smooth edges, and tell the mud puddle jumpers to land carefully in them so that they don't get hurt. Tell the water hoser to hold the hose low to the ground so that she doesn't squirt anyone in the face.

111

Watch the colors creep up the water spout.

Creeping Colors

Observe how water absorbs and spreads color.

Materials

Medium-size glass or plastic jar

Coffee filters

Paper clips

Tape

Food coloring

For Variations

3 shoelaces

Small bowls or saucers

Large jar

Flowers (light colored)

SAFETY *Make sure kids are careful with the glass containers.*

What to Do

Pour ½ inch of water into the jar. Cut four strips as long as the jar from coffee filters. Attach a paper clip to one end of the filter strip and a 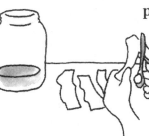 piece of tape to the other end. Place a dot of food coloring 1½ inches from the bottom of the strip, above the paper clip. Tape the strips to the top of the inside of the jar, allowing the paper clips to touch the water. Watch what happens 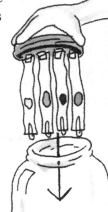 to the colored dots when the water begins to climb up the filter strips.

Variation Experiment with shoelaces instead of coffee filter strips. Get three different shoelaces—fat, thin, and medium—all made from cotton and clip off the plastic ends. Put an end of each shoelace in a bowl of water and put the other end in a small bowl or saucer. Check to see which bowl fills fastest with water.

Variation "Water" a plant with a shoelace. Fill a bowl with water and insert an end of the shoelace into the bowl. Poke the other end into the soil around a plant.

Variation You can also color flowers using this method. Fill a large jar with water and stir in several drops of food coloring. Cut flower stems at an angle and place the flowers in the jar. Watch the flowers turn color as they absorb the colored water.

CHAPTER EIGHT

Toys and water go together like kids and fun. You provide a little of both and the kids will take it from there. Water toys provide imaginary fun, manipulative challenges, and problem-solving challenges, too. Here are some water toys you can make to keep the kids entertained for hours. See "Magnifying Microscope," "Ocean Wave Bottle," "Water Clock," and "Water Whirler" for a few of our favorites.

Play water war with a Squirt Bird! By the end of the battle, everyone will have made a clean getaway.

Squirt Bird

Squirt each other and get wet.

Materials

Plastic spray bottle

Felt-tipped permanent pen

2 plastic margarine tub lids

Rubber cement or permanent glue

Food coloring

What to Do

To make your Squirt Bird, thoroughly clean a squirt bottle, or buy a new one. Dry the outside of the bottle. Draw a bird face on the handle with felt-tipped permanent pen. Cut "wings" from margarine tub lids, place them on the back of the bottle, and glue them on with rubber cement, permanent glue, or a glue gun (with grown-up help), so wings will stick out at the sides. Tint water with food coloring, flip the bottle, and squeeze the "beak" to see your Squirt Bird spray.

Variation Make several Squirt Birds and let the kids have a Squirt Bird war.

Variation Use in the bathtub so the kids have fun while they get clean.

Variation Let the kids spray the colored water on a fence and make designs. The colored water will evaporate, leaving a clean surface.

Variation Set an object on top of the fence and have the kids try to spray it off. Set up several items and let them squirt down as many as they can. Have a distance competition to see which Squirt Bird sprays the farthest.

✚ SAFETY

Make sure the bottle is completely cleaned and that it did not contain harsh chemicals, such as lye, acid, or corrosives. Tell the kids not to squirt each other in the face.

You've heard of a ship in a bottle? Here's an "ocean in a bottle." This simple, unique plaything is fun to make, and the result is a long-lasting toy that kids find fascinating for hours.

Ages: 2 and up

Ocean Wave Bottle

Make a wave in a bottle.

Materials

1 or 2 clear plastic 32-ounce soda bottles

Funnel

½ cup water

½ cup cooking oil

½ cup vinegar

Blue food coloring

Glitter, sequins, and plastic confetti

For Variations

Tornado Tube (optional)

Small plastic toy

Dish-washing liquid

Metallic confetti

Rubber cement

What to Do

Prepare the bottle by washing it, removing labels, and drying the outside. Using a funnel, pour the water into a bottle, then add the oil and vinegar. Have the kids watch to see what happens as you add the different liquids. Add several drops of blue (or other) food coloring, then add glitter, sequins, and plastic confetti. Close the cap and seal it shut with the rubber cement. Tell the kids to shake the bottles to make the waves, or swirl them around to create a tornado effect.

Variation Fill one bottle just with water. Connect two bottles together using the Tornado Tube (available from toy, hobby, and school supply stores). Watch the water funnel down from the top bottle to the bottom bottle when they are held upright and swirled gently in a circle.

Variation Add a small plastic toy along with the glitter and sequins to the oil, water, and vinegar bottle and have the kids try to find the hidden toy among the swirls. Make waves in a variety of colors using separate bottles for each color.

Variation Fill a soda bottle with water, adding 2 capfuls of dishwashing liquid and a small amount of metallic confetti. Leave 1 inch of air space at the top of the bottle. Screw on the lid tightly, then swirl the bottle to make a tornado.

SAFETY

Watch that the kids don't drink any of their concoctions. The rubber cement should be handled by grown-ups. Once the cap is secure, the toy should be safe for all ages, but watch for wear, cracks, or damage. It's not indestructible!

This toy truck is made entirely from household discards, and it really works!

Street Cleaner

Make a toy truck that squirts water.

Materials

White and red enamel spray paint

Empty cereal box, 13-ounce size

Empty adhesive-bandage box

4 jar lids, all the same size

Hammer and nail

4 paper fasteners

Clear plastic spray bottle

Food coloring

2 large rubber bands

Decals, felt-tipped permanent pens, and paint

What to Do

Spray paint the cereal box and adhesive-bandage box white. Glue the smaller box to the cereal box in an L-shape, to make a truck base and truck cab. Spray paint the lids red to make wheels. Make a small hole in the center of each lid with a hammer and nail. Make corresponding holes in the cereal box by pressing the nail through to attach the wheels. Secure wheels to the box with paper fasteners. Rinse plastic spray bottle and fill with colored water. Lay the bottle on the cereal box and secure with two large rubber bands. Add decorations to truck with felt-tipped pens, decals, and paint.

117

SAFETY

Make sure the spray bottle is thoroughly cleaned. Young children will need help and supervision with the cutting and assembly.

Variation Turn it into a fire engine by painting the entire truck red. Attach thick string to the bottle to make a "hose." Add bells for fire engine sirens that ring as you drive the truck.

Here's a "timely" idea. Create your own water clock to keep track of the minutes.

Ages: 6 and up

Water Clock

Make your own clock.

Materials

32-ounce jar (plastic preferred)

32-ounce metal can

Thin nail

Hammer

Felt-tipped permanent pen

Watch with a second hand

For Variation

Sand

What to Do

Clean out the jar and can thoroughly. Using a thin nail and a hammer, tap a tiny hole in the bottom of the can. Draw a vertical line along the side of the jar with the felt-tipped pen. Place your finger over the hole in the can and fill the can with water. Set the can on the open jar, allow the water to drip out, and begin keeping track of the time with the watch's second hand. Each time a minute passes, mark the water level on the jar with the felt-tipped pen. Empty the jar back into the can. Set the can on top of the jar again and let it drip. This time you won't need the watch. Your jar will tell you how much time has passed as it drains off the minutes.

Variation Fill the can with sand instead of water and make yourself a Sand Clock.

SAFETY

Use a plastic jar if possible, so it won't break. Be sure the can has no sharp edges. Grown–up help is necessary for hammer and nail use.

119

Impress your friends and relatives with this gravity–defying trick.
But wear your bathing suit, just in case.

Water Whirlers

Spin a bucket of water without letting the water spill.

Materials

Large plastic bucket or container (such as a margarine tub)

Thick nail

Hammer

String, 6 feet

What to Do

Clean out the plastic container. Make three holes an equal distance apart near the top of the container by carefully hammering a thick nail through the plastic. Remove nail. Cut the 6-foot string into three equal pieces, each 2 feet long. Put each piece through a hole and secure it tightly on the outside of the container with a double knot. Tie the opposite ends together. Fill the container half full with water. Go outside and spin around in a circle as fast as you can with your Water Whirler extended and show your friends that the water won't spill out.

Variation Make several Water Whirlers, give them to friends, and have a contest to see who can spin the slowest without spilling any water. Be creative in the way you whirl your Water Whirler and see what other ways you can defy gravity.

SAFETY

Be sure you whirl the water outside so the furniture doesn't get soaked. Don't let go of the strings or the bucket will go flying. Grown–up supervision is necessary when using the hammer and nail.

Create your own winter wonderland,
even in the middle of the summer.

Snow Globe

Make a snow scene in a jar.

Materials

Baby food jar

Baby oil or corn syrup

Water

Glitter, star sparkles, metallic confetti, and soap flakes (like Ivory Snow)

Glue

Tiny plastic figures

What to Do

Fill a jar with baby oil or corn syrup and a little water. Add glitter, sparkles, metallic confetti, soap flakes, or other tiny sprinkles to act as snow. Glue tiny plastic figures (use winter figures such as trees, snowmen, or Santa Claus) to the inside of the lid with permanent glue and allow to dry. Close the jar and seal the lid shut with permanent glue. Turn the jar upside down, give it a shake, and then watch the "snow" fall onto the figures.

Variation Make jars for the other three seasons. Use tiny flower petals for spring with a small flower glued to the inside of the lid, glitter for the summer sunlight with seashells glued to the lid, and tiny leaves for fall with little pumpkins or fall trees glued to the lid.

SAFETY

A glue gun makes a nice firm seal, but it should only be handled by grown-ups and used with caution around the kids. Try to use a plastic jar rather than a glass one.

Here's a fun-to-ride rickety raft to keep you wet in the water.

Ages: 8 and up

Rickety Raft

Try and stay on the raft as long as possible.

Materials

3 inner tubes

2-by-4 plank of wood a little longer than the inner tubes lined up next to each other

Sandpaper

Drill

Paint and brush

Nylon rope, 32 feet long

What to Do

Get three inner tubes and measure their length when put side by side. Buy a board a little longer, and ask the lumberyard to round the edges, if possible. If not, a grown-up can round the edges with a saw. Use sandpaper to remove sharp edges or splinters. Place the board on the ground and set the three inner tubes on top of the board, equal distance from either end and nearly touching each other. Outline the tubes on the board where they make contact and remove the tubes. Have a grown-up drill two holes on every line, equal distance from the edge of the

122

wood and one another. There should be 24 holes altogether. Sand around the holes. Paint the board and let it dry. Set the tubes on the board and lace nylon rope through the holes, over the tubes, and

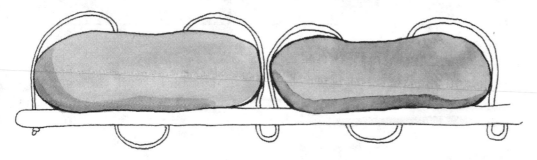

under the board to secure them to the board. Knot the ends of the ropes, turn the board over in the water with the inner tubes underneath, straddle the board, and set sail.

Variation Try to keep your balance on the rickety raft by floating on it in different ways. See how many kids the raft will hold. Make two and have a raft race, or see which team can stay on the longest.

SAFETY

Use tools with grown-up supervision and assistance. Make sure rafters can swim and don't use the raft in deep or turbulent water. To be safe in deep water, give the kids life jackets to wear.

Be creative and design your own
sailing vessel to use in the water.

Bobbing Boats

Create your own boat.

Materials

Styrofoam plates, cups, trays, cartons, milk cartons, and other floatable containers

Electrical tape

Flexible straws

Balloons, round and long

Bamboo skewers and Popsicle sticks

Sponges and corks

Fish bobbers and fishing line

Scissors, waterproof glue, string, rubber bands, and pipe cleaners

What to Do

Set up a table for the kids to work on and let them build their small boats. Provide the materials listed above and let them create whatever

they want that will float on the water. Make suggestions if they get stuck, but encourage them to be creative and design unique boats.

Variation Provide pictures of boats to stimulate the kids' imaginations. Then suggest that they build a sailing ship, a pirate ship, a sailboat, a catamaran, a power boat, a tugboat, an ocean liner, a cruise ship, Tom Sawyer's raft, a water plane, a canoe, or a submarine. You can find pictures of boats in picture books at the library.

Variation Have a boat race in the water when all the boats are finished. Or have a contest and award prizes to the funniest boat, the largest boat, the most creative boat, the most realistic boat, the boat most likely to sink, and so on. Make sure everyone wins a prize.

SAFETY

Keep an eye on the kids to make sure they don't hurt themselves with any of the materials and supervise young children carefully.

*You can see water critters up close and personal
with this homemade Magnifying Microscope.*

Magnifying Microscope

View magnified tiny water life.

Materials

Large plastic containers: potato-salad bucket, mayonnaise jar, or margarine tub

Heavy-duty plastic wrap

Pan

Large rubber band

For Variation

Small toys, plants, food, or bugs

What to Do

Cut the bottom from the plastic container. Lay a piece of plastic wrap across the opening at the top. Place a rubber band around the plastic wrap to hold it tightly in place. This is your magnifier. Now, collect a small amount of pond, creek, river, lake, or ocean water in a pan. Place the magnifier into the water and look at the water life you have captured in your pan. The pressure of the water on the wrap will cause it to enlarge the things you're looking at.

Variation Look at other things under the water, such as small toys, plants, your foot, your hair, food, or bugs.

SAFETY

Cover sharp edges on the plastic container with electrical tape.

*Beat on your water drum and listen
to the wonderful sound it makes.*

Ages: 3 and up

Water Drum

Make your own drum and hear the sounds that water makes.

Materials

Coffee can or pail

Chamois, canvas, or heavy plastic (to cover the top of the can, allowing a 1-inch overhang)

Rubber band, wire, string, or duct tape

What to Do

Fill a quarter of the can with water. Stretch chamois, canvas, or plastic (available at hardware, drug, or auto stores) over the top and secure tightly with rubber band, wire, string, or duct tape. The tighter the covering, the better the sound. Tap out a rhythm on the drums with your hands.

Variation Make a variety of drums from cans and metal containers of all sizes. Notice the differences in sound among the different sizes.

Variation Have the kids make several drums and paint them. Now they can put on a drum show. Play music on a cassette player while the kids tap out the rhythm to the tunes.

+ SAFETY

Cover sharp edges of cans and metal containers with electrical tape.

127

CHAPTER NINE

WATER GAMES

If you're looking for games to play at birthday parties, group meetings, with neighborhood kids, or your family, try some of these exciting water games. They're bound to make everyone wet, wild, and wacky. "Water Bomb Toss" is guaranteed to get them wet even when they try to stay dry, and "Wet T-shirt Race" is harder to manage than it sounds. "Splash!" is just plain fun! On your mark, get set, go!

Here's a fun game to play in the pool.

Octopus Tag

Tag another player with your toes.

Materials

Pool or lake

How to Play

Select one player to be the Poisonous Octopus while the rest are Fishes in the sea. With her hands behind her back, the Octopus tries to tag the other players using only her toes. If she touches another player, that player has been "poisoned by the Octopus' tentacles" and is "out." Continue until everyone has been tagged.

Variation When the Octopus tags another player that player becomes the Octopus. The former Octopus returns to the group and joins in the game.

Variation When the Octopus tags another player that player becomes the Octopus while the former Octopus drops out of the game. The game continues until only one player is left.

Variation Play the game with everyone's eyes closed.

Variation Tell the Fishes to see how close they can get to the Octopus without being tagged. It takes some effort to tag with the toes, so the teasing creates more of a suspenseful challenge.

SAFETY

Be sure all players are good swimmers. Play the game in the shallow end for safety.

Swimmy is running this water show,
so do what Swimmy says!

Swimmy Says

Cross the finish line by following Swimmy's instructions.

Materials

Pool, lake, or sprinkler

How to Play

This game is similar to "Mother, May I?" but this time Swimmy gives the orders, and the game is played in the water. Have all players line up at one end of the pool. Swimmy gives each player, one at a time, an instruction to follow in the water. A player

only follows the instruction when Swimmy begins, "Swimmy says . . ." If Swimmy does not say "Swimmy says," the player does not move. For example, if Swimmy says "Player One. Swimmy says, do a somersault," Player One responds, "Swimmy says so?" before he can move. If Swimmy says so, the player can complete the instruction moving closer to the other end of the pool. If Swimmy does not say so, the player does not move. If he accidentally follows the instruction, or even moves, he must return to the starting line. The first player to get to the other side of the pool becomes the new Swimmy.

Variation Play this in the backyard with the sprinklers running. Have Swimmy stand on one side of the yard and have the other players stand on the other side. Have Swimmy give them instructions causing them to move through a sprinkler. The players have to stand still at their spots and not move if it's not their turn, or if Swimmy has not said, "Swimmy says."

Variation Play the game in the pool with everyone's eyes closed. No one will know who is winning or exactly where the finish line is.

SAFETY

If they play in the pool, players should be good swimmers, since they will need to tread water, unless they play in the shallow end. If the kids close their eyes, make sure the area is safe.

It's not easy getting dressed when your clothes are wet!

Wet T-shirt Race

Team members race to the other side hindered by wet T-shirts.

Materials

2 large T-shirts

For Variations

Old pants, socks, vests, or gloves

How to Play

Divide the players into two teams and divide the teams in half, with each half facing each other on opposite sides of the pool or swimming area. Give the first player on each team a wet T-shirt. On the word "Go!" the first players on one side race to put on the wet T-shirt. When the shirts are on, they must jump into the pool and swim to the other side, get out of the pool, and remove the wet T-shirt. The second player takes the wet shirt and puts it on, then jumps into the pool and races for the other side. The team that completes the race first wins a wet T-shirt. Watch the fun as the players try to put on and take off their wet T-shirts.

Variation Do the same with pants, socks, vests, or gloves, one at a time.

Variation If they're playing in the shallow end, have the kids put on all the clothes before they race across to the other side. They should be able to cross by walking, not swimming, since the wet clothes may weigh them down too much to be in the deep end and try to swim.

SAFETY

Do not have the kids dress in all the clothes at once if they are swimming in the deep end. Make sure the kids are good swimmers.

*Plan to get wet—that's the idea behind
this exciting, tension-filled game!*

Ages: 4 and up

Players: 4 or more

Water Bomb Toss

Successfully toss a water balloon back and forth without letting it break.

Materials

Water balloons

How to Play

Fill balloons with water and have plenty on hand. They break easily and the kids are going to want to play this game several times. Line up the players in two lines facing each other and about 2 feet apart. Give one line of players one water balloon each. When you say "Toss!" the players with the water balloons must toss them gently to their partners. If everyone successfully completes the toss, have the players step back one foot. Then say "Toss!" again and have them toss the balloons back to their partners. If everyone is still dry and no balloons have popped have them step farther and farther apart after every toss. When someone finally misses the catch, tosses too hard, or accidentally pops a balloon and gets splashed, that team drops out of the game and the rest continue until all have popped their balloons. Repeat the game with fresh balloons.

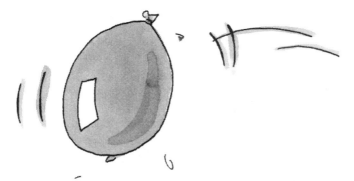

Variation Give the players obstacles to overcome while they play. Have them toss the balloons backward or under their legs. They might also try tossing them blindfolded, tossing and catching with one hand overhand or underhand, and spinning and throwing them high in the air.

SAFETY

Tell the kids not to throw the balloons hard, especially at other players' faces, so they won't get hurt. Warn the kids that they will get wet and that they should wear appropriate clothing.

Aye, matey, your ship's sinking fast! You've got to get the water
out before the S.S. Minnow sinks to the bottom! S.O.S.!

Ages: 6 and up

Players: 4 or more

Sinking Ship

Be the first to fill your bucket with water.

Materials
2 pails or buckets

For Variations
Paper plates

How to Play

Divide up teams and have each team line up at one side of the shallow end of a pool or lake. Set out two small, empty pails on the other side of the pool (clear plastic buckets or tubs work best because it's easy to see the water level). On the call of "S.O.S.!" the first players on each team scoop up a handful of water and attempt carry it to the other side of the pool or lake. Then they pour what's left of the water into the bucket and run back to the team and tag the next players, who must do the same thing. The bucket that fills up first, wins.

Variation Have the players raise their arms over their heads to carry the water. Or have them carry the water with paper plates or large spoons, or put one hand behind their backs when they carry the paper plates.

Variation Play the game in the kiddie pool or use sprinklers. Have the kids fill their hands or paper plates with water from the sprinklers and run to buckets several feet away.

SAFETY

Keep the game in the shallow end for safety.

136

You never know when the dam will break and the water will overflow.
The surprise is what makes this game so much fun.

Ages: 3 and up

Players: 5 or more

Get the player who splashes you.

Materials

Plastic cups

How to Play

Have the players sit in a circle on the lawn in their bathing suits. Fill a bucket with water and set it in the middle of the circle. Select one player to be Splash Maker and give her the plastic cup. Have her scoop a cup full of water from the bucket, and carry it outside the circle of players. Splash Maker walks around the outside of the circle with the cup of water. As she passes the players, she calls out their names until finally, instead of calling out a name, she calls out "Splash!"—and pours a cup of water over a player. The wet player jumps up and runs after Splash Maker, who runs around the circle and tries to sit in the wet player's seat. If she makes it, the wet player becomes Splash Maker. If she is tagged by the wet player, she must be Splash Maker again.

Variation Play a version of Blindman's Bluff with the hose. Have the kids stand in a line. Have a player stand opposite the line holding the hose. The hoser must close her eyes and count to 10 while the other kids scramble around the yard, still in plain sight, but in new spots. When the hoser reaches 10, keeping her eyes closed, the other players must freeze where they are. The hoser turns the hose on and waves it around, trying to tag the other players. The first player who is squirted by the hose must leave the playing area, and the play continues until there is only one player left.

Variation Give every player a cup of water. Have Splash Maker walk around the outside of the circle with her cup of water. When she finally dumps it on a player that player must try to splash her back with his cup of water.

137

*Will you ever be able to capture Jaws alive? Just
when you least expect it, Jaws "pops" again.*

Volley Jaws

*Get Jaws into the center of the inner tube before
the other team does—and before Jaws pops!*

Materials

Balloons

Inner tube

Black felt-tipped
permanent pen

How to Play

Divide the players into two teams and have them get on either side of
an inner tube that is floating in the center of the pool or lake. Draw a
Jaws face on an inflated balloon with a felt-tipped pen and toss it to
the crowd. Have each team try to dunk the balloon into the center of
the inner tube before the other team, by passing it around like a basketball or volleyball. If "Jaws" pops, the team responsible loses a point
and the other team gains possession of "Jaws II." Play resumes until
someone dunks Jaws into the center of the inner tube and scores a
point or Jaws pops again. Since the balloon is fragile and the inner
tube is always moving around, this is a fun, fast-moving game.

SAFETY

This is a rough game. Make sure the sides are equal and all the players are good swimmers.

Variation Make the game confusing by adding a bunch of inflated, colored balloons in the pool, and make the Jaws balloon white with a face.

Variation If you don't like the popping, use a large plastic ball and just try to sink it into the floating inner tube.

Sharp ears and quiet strokes are key components in this scary alligator game. Don't get caught or you may end up as a handbag.

Ages: 6 and up

Players: 4 or more

Alligator Escape

Escape the alligator and get to the other side of the lagoon.

How to Play

Pick a category, such as colors, and let everyone pick a color except the Alligator, who stands apart from the group with his ears plugged. After all the players have quietly chosen different colors, have them line up in the water along one end of the pool or lake, preferably at the deep end. The Alligator stands outside the water at the same end of the pool with his back to the players and begins to call out the names of colors, pausing between each color to listen for the rustle of the water. When a player hears her color called by the Alligator, she must immediately start swimming for the other end of the pool. If the Alligator hears her swimming, she may turn around, jump into the pool, chase the swimmer, and attempt to tag her. If the swimmer is tagged, she becomes the Alligator. If she makes it to the other end, the Alligator again stands out of the water and calls other colors. The game is over when someone is caught by the hungry Alligator.

Variation Try a variety of categories and change them each time you play. Other categories you may choose are cars, candy bars, school subjects, girls' or boys' names, TV shows, musical groups, articles of clothing, snack foods, types of drinks, animals, flowers, and trees.

*Have an underwater adventure with
old golf balls and plastic bottles!*

Ages: 8 and up

Players: 2 or more

Swim the underwater adventure course as fast as possible.

Materials

10 empty plastic bottles with handles and caps

Felt-tipped permanent pen

Nylon rope

10 heavy rocks, 10 golf balls or small, painted rocks

For Variation

Frisbees or small plastic rings

How to Play

Clean the bottles and peel off labels. Number the bottles from 1 to 10 using the felt-tipped permanent pen. Measure the rope from the surface of the water to the bottom, allow extra length for tying, and cut 10 lengths. Tie one end of each rope to the handle of a bottle and tie the other end to a heavy rock. Sink the rock to the bottom, allowing the bottle to float at the top. Repeat for the rest of the bottles and scatter them throughout the pool or lake. Place a golf ball or a painted rock next to each anchored rock at the bottom of the pool. Then race to collect the golf balls or painted rocks from each of the floating markers.

Variation Play Water Frisbee Golf using floaters instead of anchors. Float the bottles throughout the pool or lake area. From the edge of the pool or from the previous numbered floater, toss a Frisbee or a small plastic ring around the next numbered bottle. Take turns as in golf, and count how many times it takes to loop the bottle. When all have scored, move on to the next bottle.

SAFETY

This game is only for good swimmers. Don't play it in very deep water.

An underwater game of name that tune—and more!

Ages: 8 and up

Players: 2 or more

Submarine Sonar

Try to understand what others are singing or saying underwater.

What to Do

No special talent is required for this musical marine game. Have all the kids duck underwater for a few seconds at a time. Each time they go under, one sings a favorite tune for the others. The others must guess the name of the song. Whoever guesses the song gets to be the next singer.

Variation Make different noises, like animal sounds, car sounds, beeps, sneezes, laughter, moaning, screams, or bubbles. Have the others listen. When all players come to the surface, one of the other players reproduces the sounds he thinks he heard underwater.

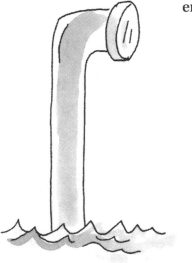

142

Variation Say simple sentences underwater. When everyone comes up for air, have the others repeat the sentences. Or play Telephone underwater by having two players duck under the water. Have one player say something to the other. Then have the other player duck under the water with a third player and repeat what she thinks the first player said. Repeat until all the players have heard the sentence. Have the last player say out loud what he heard. See how it compares to the original sentence.

SAFETY

Remind the kids to come up frequently for air.

CHAPTER TEN

WATER ARTS & CRAFTS

Water can be used for lots of arts-and-crafts activities. With its unique properties and changeable shape, it can turn plain old paper into a work of art, wax into wondrous candles, and paint into dazzling displays of color. Watch what happens to chalk when you mix it with water to make a "chalk melt." Or make a "water sculpture" that changes each time you work. Have fun with "sponge paintings" that take you beyond the usual paintbrush art. Or surprise even Mother Nature with a "rainy daze" creation.

With water arts and crafts, you can make the world a prettier place. And it all begins with water!

Color and clean at the same time? Try these soap-and-water crayons and see!

Soap & Water Crayons

Make your own soap crayons.

Materials

1 cup soap flakes (like Ivory Snow)

Mixing bowl

Muffin tin

For Variation

Electric or manual mixer

Large sheets of paper

¼ cup warm water

Food coloring

SAFETY

Be careful that the soap doesn't get in the kids' eyes.

What to Do

Measure soap flakes into a mixing bowl. Add warm water and mix well. Scoop mixture into muffin-tin cups. Add several drops of food coloring to each cup, making each one a different color. Mix a couple of colors together to create a new color. Stir each cup well, until blended. Allow to dry two to three days. Pop the mixture from the cups when it is firm. Use to color on paper, skin, or any other surface. The color washes off with water.

Variation Whip soap flakes with water and food coloring in a mixing bowl with an electric or manual mixer. (Kids will need grown-up help.) Add water as needed. When the mixture is light and fluffy, let the kids "paint" with the colored snow puffs on large sheets of paper, on the sidewalk, or on themselves in the bathtub.

A new way to paint using a secret ingredient: water.

Squeeze Paint

Experience a new way of painting.

Materials

2 cups flour

½ cup salt

½ cup sugar

1½ cups water

4 plastic squeeze bottles (like ketchup or shampoo bottles)

Food coloring

Spoon

White construction paper

For Variations

Paintbrushes

Sprinkles, glitter, sand, or metallic confetti

What to Do

Combine flour, salt, sugar, and water and mix well. Separate mixture into four bottles. Add food coloring to each bottle to make red, blue, yellow, and green paint. Stir with a spoon, then replace top and shake well. Give the kids the bottles of paint and several large sheets of white construction paper. Let kids squeeze on a design and allow to dry. Paint will dry like thick glue.

Variation Have the kids squeeze-paint a design on just half of the large sheet of paper. When they are finished, fold the paper in half, press down on it, then open it to reveal a mirror-like design.

Variation Have the kids squeeze out a small glob of paint, then give them paintbrushes to spread the paint on the paper.

Variation Add sprinkles, glitter, sand, metallic confetti, or other items to decorate the paint after it has been squeezed onto the paper.

SAFETY

This is a messy activity so cover your work space well. Use squeeze bottles with tiny openings so the paint won't come out too fast and tell the kids to squeeze out the paint slowly.

A new way to express yourself—with sponges.

Sponge Painting

Color on paper with sponges.

Materials

Scissors

Sponges or foam

Tempera paint

Water

Flat saucers or dishes

Construction paper

What to Do

Use scissors to cut sponges into interesting shapes. You might cut out alphabet letters, numbers, geometric shapes, animals, spaceships, or whatever your child likes. You can also use foam instead of sponges; it is available at hardware, craft, and fabric stores in large sheets. Dilute liquid tempera paint with water. Pour small amounts of different colors in saucers. Let the kids press the sponges into the saucers of paint, then onto large sheets of construction paper to make designs. Have them write their names, create landscapes, or tell a story with their sponge shapes.

Variation Have the kids repeat the same shapes over and over to make wrapping paper. Or make greeting cards, picture frames, or place mats.

SAFETY

Tell kids to keep sponges on the paper. Keep the activity contained at a table covered with

Water works wonders on a substance like chalk.
Get your chalk wet and see what happens.

Chalk Melt

Ages: 3 and up

Feel the chalk "melt" as you draw a design.

Materials

Colored chalk

Pan of water

Slick white paper

For Variation

Sugar

What to Do

Soak colored chalk in a pan of water for 5 to 10 minutes. Remove chalk. Get slick white paper (other paper is fine but slick paper works best) and dip the paper into the pan of water, or run it under the faucet. Set it on the table with newspapers underneath, and let the kids draw on the wet paper with the wet chalk. Keep the pan of water nearby for dipping chalk. It's a whole new experience!

Variation Add sugar to the water to give it an interesting texture. Mix well so the sugar is completely dissolved, then let the kids dip their chalk into the sugar water.

Variation Let the kids draw on a wet sidewalk with wet chalk. They can make giant monsters, whole cities, or write their names. When they're finished with their artwork, hose off the surface to clean it up.

SAFETY

This is a messy activity so keep newspapers handy and have the kids wear old clothes.

This technique gives pictures a luminescent look. Watch the delighted faces of the kids as their artwork comes to life under the watercolors.

Ages: 4 and up

Water Art

Use crayons and watercolors together for a special effect.

Materials

Newspapers

White construction paper

Crayons

Plastic spray bottle

Watercolors

Paintbrushes

For Variations

Tempera paint

Straw

What to Do

Lay out materials on a table covered with newspapers. Give each child a large sheet of white construction paper and set out a box of crayons for everyone to use. Have the kids color their pictures with crayons, leaving some white space in their designs. When they're finished, use a plastic spray bottle to spray the paper with water. Give the kids watercolors and paintbrushes to paint over the picture and watch the paint bleed over the white spaces and crayon designs. When the pictures are finished, allow them to dry and admire the results.

Variation Put globs of diluted tempera paint on the paper. Let the kids spray the globs with the spray bottle to create interesting designs.

Variation Dip a straw into a bottle of diluted tempera paint. Close off the top of the straw with one finger and lift it out again. Place the paint-filled straw over a sheet of white paper and let your finger off, allowing the paint to drop onto the paper. Give your child the straw and have him blow the glob of paint in several directions on the paper. Watch the fascinating effects.

SAFETY

Remind the kids not to inhale the paint in the straw.

You'll need a rainy day for this art project.

Rainy Daze

See what rain can do to the paint.

Materials

Food coloring or poster paint

White paper plate

For Variations

Colored chalk

Dry poster paint

Plastic spray bottle

What to Do

Place a few drops of food coloring or poster paint on a white paper plate (not plastic). Keep the drops separate around the plate. Hold the plate outside in the rain and watch the rainwater "paint" a picture. Let the colors run together to create an interesting design. Then bring the plate inside and let it dry. When it's dry, you can hang it on the refrigerator or use it for a lunch plate, if you painted with food coloring.

Variation Draw a picture with colored chalk and do the same with rainwater. Then watch the rain melt and soften the design.

Variation Sprinkle dry poster paint in various sections of the paper plate. Hold it out in the rain and watch the water melt and blend the once-dry paints.

Variation If it's not a rainy day, use a spray bottle filled with water to get a similar effect. Let the colors run together and see the design that appears.

SAFETY

If it's a cold, rainy day and you don't want the kids outside, open a window and hang the plate outside.

151

*This fascinating water sculpture will keep
the kids mesmerized for hours.*

Ages: 4 and up

Water Sculpture

See what happens when oil and water are mixed together.

Materials

Plastic or glass jar with lid

Food coloring

Mineral or vegetable oil

For Variation

Glitter or sequins

What to Do

Find a large plastic or glass jar, clean it thoroughly, and remove labels. Make sure the lid fits tightly at the top. Fill the jar halfway with water. Add several drops of food coloring. Then fill the jar the rest of the way with oil, pouring slowly. Screw the lid on tight and make sure there's no leakage. Then hold the jar sideways and roll it back and forth to create the water sculpture. Watch how the substance moves, changes, and swirls, but never really combines.

Variation Add glitter or sequins to the water.

SAFETY

Try to use a plastic jar so you won't worry about breakage. Make sure the lid seals tightly.

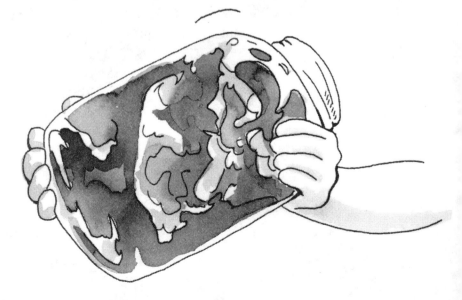

152

Make your own tie-dye picture using this easy method.

Rainbow Tie-Dye

Watch the colors blend on the coffee filters.

Materials

4 small bowls of water

Food coloring

Coffee filters

Rubber gloves

Newspaper

For Variations

Porous white paper (tissue paper or paper napkins)

White crayon

What to Do

Fill small bowls with 1 cup water each. Pour 2 or 3 teaspoons of food coloring into each bowl and stir. Crumple a coffee filter tightly into a ball. Put on rubber gloves if you don't want to color your hands. Dip part of the filter into a bowl of dye and watch it absorb the color. Remove and squeeze out the excess dye. Dip another section of the filter into another color. Squeeze out excess dye and repeat for remaining two colors. When completely colored, flatten the filter on newspaper and allow it to dry.

Variation You can use tissue paper, paper napkins, or any other porous white paper. You don't have to squeeze out the excess color if you don't want to. The filter will just take a little longer to dry.

Variation Using a white crayon, draw a design around the coffee filter. Crinkle the filter and dip it into food coloring, then flatten on newspaper to dry.

SAFETY

The food coloring will temporarily dye your hands. To prevent this from happening wear gloves.

*An interesting way to make your own icicles,
but you'll need a very cold day.*

Ages: 6 and up

Crystal Art

See the crystals form.

Materials
Plastic container

Tack or pin

String

For Variation
Food coloring

Fruit-flavored drink

What to Do

Find a plastic container (a large margarine tub works well) and punch a very small hole using a tack or pin near the bottom edge. If the hole is too small, the water won't drip out fast enough, but if it's too big, it will drip out too fast, so you may have to experiment with different-size holes. Punch three larger holes through the top of the container to form a triangle and thread string through holes. Tie string together, hang from a tree on a below-freezing day or night, and fill the container with water. As the water drips out slowly and freezes, it will create an icicle. Refill as needed.

Variation Make several tiny holes at the bottom to create a bunch of icicles. Fill the container with water and a few drips of food coloring to make colorful icicles. Or fill it with fruit-flavored drink to make your own icicle Popsicles.

SAFETY

Grown-ups should punch holes in the container.

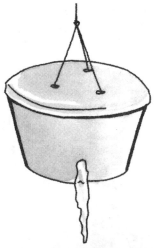

154

*Do fire and ice go together? This time they do,
for an unusual and beautiful effect.*

Fire & Ice Candles

Create unusual candles using ice.

Materials

Playdoh or clay

Quart-size milk carton

Old candle

1 package paraffin (available at hobby and hardware stores)

Large coffee can

Crayons

Pot holders

Ice

What to Do

Place a ball of Playdoh or clay at the bottom of the milk carton. Insert an old candle into the clay in the milk carton, and trim the milk carton to a few inches taller than the old candle. Melt paraffin in a coffee can set in a pan of water and heat until melted. Add peeled crayons of similar colors to the wax and stir in to melt. Carefully remove wax from heat, holding the can with pot holders. Place coarsely crushed ice around the old candle in the milk carton, filling it to the top. Carefully pour in paraffin. The wax will harden as the ice melts, creating unusual holes like Swiss cheese in the wax. When the wax is cool, pour off water, peel off milk carton, and enjoy your new Fire and Ice Candle.

Variation Layer broken crayons with the ice, then pour wax over. This creates a textured design when the ice melts, leaving the wax with the crayons "floating" inside. Or add other nonflammable items around the ice, such as beads and faux jewelry, to create a fancy candle.

SAFETY

Use extreme caution with hot wax. Grown-ups should handle the paraffin from start to finish.

Kids' Activity Books the Whole Family Can Enjoy

Big Book of Fun
Creative Learning Activities for Home & School,
Ages 4–12
Carolyn Buhai Haas
Illustrated by Jane Bennet Phillips
Includes more than 200 projects and activities—
from indoor-outdoor games and nature crafts to
holiday ideas, cooking fun, and much more.
ISBN 1-55652-020-4
280 pages, paper, $11.95

Frank Lloyd Wright For Kids
Kathleen Thorne-Thomsen
A thorough biography is followed by stimulating
projects that enable kids to grasp the ideas
underlying Wright's work—and have fun in the
process.
ages 8 & up-
ISBN 1-55652-207-X
144 pages, paper, $14.95

Green Thumbs
A Kid's Activity Guide to Indoor and Outdoor
Gardening
Laurie Carlson
With a few seeds, some water and soil, and this
book, kids will be creating gardens of their own
in no time. They will also create compost, make
watering cans, mix up bug sprays, lay slug traps,
grow crazy cucumbers, and much more.
ages 3–9
ISBN 1-55652-238-X
144 pages, paper, $12.95

Happy Birthday, Grandma Moses
Activities for Special Days Throughout the Year
Clare Bonfanti Braham and Maria Bonfanti
Esche
Illustrations by Mary Jones
The significance of 100 different celebratory
days is thoroughly explained as 200 related
activities pay charming, educational tribute to
the holidays, history, and accomplishments of
many cultures and many people.
ages 3–9
ISBN 1-55652-226-6
228 pages, paper, $11.95

Huzzah Means Hooray
Activities from the Days of Damsels, Jesters, and
Blackbirds in a Pie
Laurie Carlson
Kids can re-create a long-ago world of kings, cas-
tles, jousts, jesters, magic fairies, and Robin
Hood—all they need are their imaginations and
materials they can find at home.
ages 3–9
ISBN 1-55652-227-4
184 pages, paper, $12.95

Kids Camp!
Activities for the Backyard or Wilderness
Laurie Carlson and Judith Dammel
Young campers will build an awareness of the
environment, learn about insect and animal
behavior, boost their self-esteem, and acquire all
the basic skills for fun, successful camping.
ages 4–12
ISBN 1-55652-237-1
176 pages, paper, $12.95

Look at Me

Creative Learning Activities for Babies and Toddlers

Carolyn Buhai Haas

Illustrated by Jane Bennett Phillips

Activities for babies and toddlers that inspire creativity and learning through play.

ISBN 1-55652-021-2

228 pages, paper, $11.95

Messy Activities and More

Virginia K. Morin

Illustrated by David Sokoloff

Foreword by Ann M. Jernberg

Encourages adults and children to have fun making a mess with more than 160 interactive games and projects.

ages 3–10

ISBN 1-55652-173-1

144 pages, paper, $9.95

More Than Moccasins

A Kid's Activity Guide to Traditional North American Indian Life

Laurie Carlson

Kids will discover traditions and skills handed down from the people who first settled this continent, including how to plant a garden, make useful pottery, and communicate through Navajo code talkers.

"As an educator who works with Indian children I highly recommend [More Than Moccasins] for all kids and teachers ... I learned things about our Indian world I did not know."

—Bonnie Jo Hunt

Wicahpi Win (Star Woman)

Standing Rock Lakota

ages 3–9

ISBN 1-55652-213-4

200 pages, paper, $12.95

My Own Fun

Creative Learning Activities for Home and School

Carolyn Buhai Haas and Anita Cross Friedman

More than 160 creative learning projects and activities for elementary-school children.

ages 7–12

ISBN 1-55652-093-X

194 pages, paper, $9.95

Sandbox Scientist

Real Science Activities for Little Kids

Michael E. Ross

Illustrated by Mary Anne Lloyd

Parents, teachers, and day-care leaders learn to assemble "Explorer Kits" that will send kids off on their own investigations, in groups or individually, with a minimum of adult intervention.

ages 2–8

ISBN 1-55652-248-7

208 pages, paper, $12.95

These books are available through your local bookstore or directly from Independent Publishers Group, 814 N. Franklin Street, Chicago, Illinois 60610, 1-800-888-4741. Visa and MasterCard accepted.